Advance Praise for New Sales Speak

"Whether you are selling a tangible product, intangible service, yourself or simply an idea, *New Sales Speak* will make you a more effective communicator. With Terri's guidance you will become a better presenter . . . think about it . . . people with strong presentation skills *are* successful."

Jerry Anderson, CCIM
President, Coldwell Banker Commercial

"Terri has done a terrific job of translating the challenging and sometimes intimidating task of selling into a formula that is as simple as one, two, three. This book is not just for sales professionals, because everybody is selling something. It takes the mystery out of people's successes and failures, from the cold call to the board room, and I recommend it for anyone that will be giving presentations of any size."

Jay J. Cohen, MD, MBA
President,
Physician WebLink of California

New Sales Speak

TERRI L. SJODIN, CSP

John Wiley & Sons, Inc.

New York ▪ Chichester ▪ Weinheim ▪ Brisbane ▪ Singapore ▪ Toronto

Library of Congress Cataloging-in-Publication Data:
Sjodin, Terri L.
    New sales speak/Terri L. Sjodin.
        p.   cm.
    Includes index.
        ISBN 0-471-39570-6 (pbk. : alk. paper)
        1. Sales presentations.   I. Title
    HF5438.8.P74 256 2001
    658.85—dc21   00-043377

Printed in the United States of America.

10   9   8   7   6   5   4   3   2   1

To my dear and trusted friend, Mary Jo Standley,
who for nearly 10 years has worked as my national
program coordinator at Sjodin Communications.
I couldn't have asked for a more talented or
loyal person to help me realize my dreams.

Contents

Foreword

I f one thing is clear about life, it is that every one of us has an unimaginable amount of potential. What is also clear is that for many people that potential is barely realized even by the time we reach full stride in our careers and personal lives. Either we don't define our goals or we don't take the measured steps necessary to achieve them. I frequently ask myself what the world would be like if more people reached their potential and did so at an earlier age. With the *Chicken Soup for the Soul*® series, we are attempting to change the world one story at a time. With current sales of 60 million plus copies—33 consecutive *New York Times* best-sellers—we think we are moving people in a direction of realizing their personal potential. Our goal was and remains to inspire people to greatness, and, based on the feedback we have received so far, we believe we have touched the lives and hearts of countless individuals.

Inspiring people to greatness is one component in the equation, and giving them the tools and techniques they need to achieve their personal potential is another. That is why when Terri told me she was writing a book on the marriage between public speaking and professional selling I agreed to write the Foreword. *New Sales Speak* could easily serve as a companion to the *Chicken Soup for the Soul*® series because it shows us actually *how* to realize our dreams of greatness. It presents us with a blueprint of what to do to actually get what we want. It literally teaches us how to craft a persuasive argument and how to present it. Terri's brightness and insight radiate through on every page of her book and will help you get where you want to go. For everyone who has been inspired to achieve more from life, *New Sales Speak* is the manual that teaches us how to present ourselves in a way so we can achieve our personal goals.

My own selling career started when I was just nine years old. Mark was my name, and greeting cards were my game! I couldn't sleep at night for the vision of a shiny red bicycle my father forbade me to have unless I bought it myself. You might say I was "inspired." I had the motivation, but I was clearly lacking in the skills department. The only training I got was from my well-meaning mother, who told me, "Just be sure to smile." Not bad advice, when you think about it, but hardly a manual on sales techniques. Unfortunately, *New Sales Speak* wasn't around to jump-start my career; if it had been, I would have become the country's top greeting card salesperson far earlier than I eventually did. Just imagine if all children today were taught how to speak and sell more effectively; wouldn't that raise the bar on their future potential!

I personally believe everyone needs to learn how to build a persuasive case and deliver it with style, because everyone sells something. It doesn't matter if you are a doctor, a lawyer, or a dentist—you are selling yourself and your services every day. Having good sales skills builds confidence and self-esteem, and promotes a positive self-image—things all of us need throughout our lives. I have learned that life is about two things: relationships and communication. If you master both, life will be a beautiful, smooth sail on the lake. Fail to master them, and you will spend more time than you care to trying to resolve ensuing problems. *New Sales Speak* provides us with the tools to help us develop in both these crucial areas.

What Terri has done is to clarify the important relationship between selling and speaking. When you speak, you can reach the core of a person's soul and awaken that person to his or her true potential. Knowing both how to speak well and how to sell gives us tremendous power. With that combined knowledge, we have the means to persuade and can obtain the support of others who influence life's resources. Acquiring the skills set forth in *New Sales Speak*—

selling and speaking as a true professional—will not only help us achieve those dreams emanating from our basic need to survive, but literally give us the ability to achieve far more than we ever dreamed possible.

As we move into this new millennium, we need to reinvent ourselves. The problems of our shrinking world demand our attention as never before. We need to harness the full potential of everyone alive. Regardless of what we have achieved in the past, we need to do more in the future. No matter what we have accomplished, there are always larger ideas, bigger goals, and more influential partners with whom we can team to get the job done—and looking around, there is plenty that needs to get done. Knowing how to sell our ideas is key to making it happen and a way to leverage our resources so that together we can build a better world, one we will be proud to pass on to our children.

—MARK VICTOR HANSEN

Acknowledgments

I would like to extend my deepest gratitude and sincere appreciation to the following individuals who have helped make this book possible.

My editor, Chris Smith, principal at CC Communications in Laguna Hills, California, has been indispensable in bringing this book to life. Chris and I have worked together on three major projects during the past decade, and his experience and editorial talents constantly impress me.

Mentors Jerry Anderson, Bill Gray, Harvey Mackay, Nido Qubein, and Floyd Wickman were generous enough to share with me the pearls of wisdom that took them a lifetime to learn. I would not be where I am today without their guidance and support.

My parents, Jan and Pete Sjodin, my sister, Kim, and the rest of my wonderful and loving family have supported me through the tough times as well as the good years. Were all families as wonderful as mine, the world would be a different place.

The close circle of friends who have helped further my career and made it possible to produce another book by filling in when needed at trade shows, seminars, and during periods of heavy work deserve special recognition. These are my "no-matter-what" friends who have blessed me with their love, advice, counsel, and support: Colette Carlson, Greg Dell, Suzie Detro-Ingle, Janice Gaski, Peter Huber, Nicole Najoan, Renee Raithel, Patti Scoma, Nick Taylor, and Jason Tillery.

Acknowledgments

I would also like to express my deep appreciation to the many corporations, associations, and individuals who have included my programs in their training and development agendas. And a very special thanks goes to my colleagues and friends with the National Speakers Association. I continue to learn with them and from them. Without them, this book would not have been possible.

Introduction

From the errors of others, the wise man corrects his own.
—Publilius Syrus

With a little practice, you can develop dazzling presentations that are truly memorable. While each of us is blessed with a different level of talent, speaking ability is a learned skill, so don't think for a minute that either you have it or you don't. You can *learn* it!

New Sales Speak focuses on how to present and sell in the new millennium. We will examine the most common pitfalls people make when giving sales presentations, and I will reveal not only the mistakes, but also the effective ways to build and deliver a more effective presentation. In addition to helping you determine what kinds of information to use, I will show you how to deliver it in a way that is timely and entertaining. The more entertaining your presentation, the more information your listeners will absorb, and the greater the chances they will take action on what you say.

Sales Professionals Are Made—Not Born!

The best salespeople always have had terrific skills of persuasion. It isn't true, however, that these individuals have some God-given gift that others don't possess. Sales professionals are made, not born! The sayings "He could sell ice cubes to Eskimos," or "He could talk the birds out of the trees," are phrases used to describe the accomplishments of the most gifted sales professionals, but selling really is all

1

about training. It is a skill requiring practice, and good presenters are made—not born!

If you are like most business and professional people, you are constantly looking for opportunities to further your career and increase your income. You may have mapped out where you want to go in life, but you often don't know how to get there. Even if you are locked into regular annual raises, you know you could always earn a little more money by being promoted or perhaps even changing jobs. Although your skills are first class, it may be that someone less qualified is seizing opportunities that rightfully should be yours. The difference between profiting from those opportunities versus missing them is often the ability to sell yourself and your ideas.

If you can take all the information that is available to people today and extract those portions that are important to your listeners, and if you can get your audience to take action based on the information you are presenting, you will be far ahead of your competition. Because of their lack of training and skills, most people are afraid to give a presentation. Many doors and opportunities will open to you when people realize you have these skills and can employ them effectively.

Everybody Sells Something

Whether you are a CEO, engineer, firefighter, teacher, or sales professional, the ability to persuade individuals to believe you, then act on what you are saying, is critical to your success and central to your economic well-being. No matter who you are, you have something to sell. Frequently, in the course of your career you will be called upon to sell either yourself or your ideas. Whether you are selling yourself in an interview for a job, or selling a product, service, philosophy, or idea—everybody sells something!

Perhaps engineers constitute the least sales- and promotion-oriented group I know. Engineers like to rely on facts, numbers, and technology to lead people toward making the right decisions. Yet they still have to sell. If you need to convince a board of directors, company president, or your supervisor why a project needs more funding, additional support, or even more time, you have a selling job ahead of you.

The most common form of selling today may be simply finding a job. Even firefighters have to go through a series of in-depth interviews in which they are probed on why they should be selected over hundreds of other candidates applying for the same position. These men and women have to explain why they would be assets to the department. This process is repeated each time they seek a departmental promotion—all the way up to battalion chief. Whether you are applying for a college internship or your first job out of school, you have to know how to sell yourself and your ideas. Just getting in the door for an interview frequently requires you to justify why people should bother talking to you.

Supplementing Inadequate Training

This book is written for business and professional people as well as for those in the selling profession. It assumes a rudimentary knowledge of sales techniques. It is ironic that many sales professionals, before they are sent into the field, are given precious little presentation skills training. They receive more information than they—or their customers— would ever want to know about the product. They are briefed with videos and other colorful media about the company's founding and subsequent expansion, and they always are shown how to complete an order form. Frequently, however, that is the extent of it. Either they sink or swim.

Managers often come to me when they have a problem. Because of a glaring absence in our educational system, most people leave school without the ability to sell themselves, much less sell a product or service. Therefore, it isn't uncommon for a manager's sales team to be put through sales training and product familiarization classes. But the salespeople aren't confident about communicating information in a way that will result in their customers taking action.

Learning to Build a Persuasive Case

The solution is for the sales professional to learn how to build a persuasive case. You have to deliver the case with savvy and then have the energy, enthusiasm, creativity, and timing to complete the sale. This book is about how to develop and employ those skills so you can take advantage of opportunities. It is a refinement of the basic art of selling; but if you have already learned to walk, get ready, because now you are going to learn how to run like a champion! You will soon learn how to speak and present with more control, poise, distinction, and effectiveness.

This book is also written for anyone who gives one-on-one presentations, whether you are a company manager, teacher, or community volunteer. A speech doesn't require a large audience. It can be, and often is, delivered to an individual. If you want to know how to become more effective at selling your ideas (and who doesn't?), you will learn a great deal by reading this book. For people who prize their careers and realize the critical importance of being able to communicate ideas as a means to promotion, *New Sales Speak* will be an invaluable resource. Effective public speaking is the measure of every modern executive.

Self-Evaluation Chart and Sample Outline

Managers can use the self-evaluation chart I have included to gauge progress achieved by their sales teams. Or you can even use this presentation evaluation chart for performing your own self-evaluation to measure progress as you improve your technique. Also included is what many readers report is one of the most useful tools in actually building a persuasive presentation—a detailed sample outline. It notes specific things to look for and what tendencies to avoid.

As far as I am aware, no one has taken the principles of debate as taught in the academic environment and applied them to a selling environment. This book is unique because it focuses on persuasive messages. There is a big difference between general presenting and building a persuasive case. There are many books on public speaking and numerous books on sales. There are plenty that tell you what to say. This one teaches you how to say it. It teaches you how to present like a debater with polished public speaking skills, then apply these skills to your specific sales presentation. Persuasive public speaking is the ability to take a large amount of information and use it effectively.

These principles may best be taught by pointing out what not to do. Following is a list of the nine biggest presentation mistakes professionals make—and the ones we are going to show you how to avoid:

1. Winging it.
2. Being far too informative rather than persuasive.
3. Misusing your allotted time.
4. Providing inadequate support.
5. Failing to close the sale.
6. Being boring, boring, boring.
7. Overreliance on visual aids.
8. Distracting, annoying body language.
9. Inappropriate dress.

How to Transform Fear into Energy

In order to become a dazzling presenter and more effective salesperson, there are several things you will likely have to overcome. The biggest one is fear. Survey respondents cite speaking before a group as the activity they dread most. I will share with you ideas on how to channel your fear into energy through identifying its causes.

If you already have been giving presentations, you may have to overcome a few bad habits that are deeply ingrained. Relinquishing these can be difficult when we perceive them as part of our personalities. To improve our presentation means that we must set higher goals for ourselves. We must give up our comfortable attitude of just getting by.

Consider that you always remember the great presenter,

and you never forget the terrible presenter. Who is it that we *do* forget? We quickly forget the person who gives a mediocre or average presentation. Giving a solid, persuasive talk is challenging. If it were easy, everyone would be doing it. One reason why it can be so rewarding is that everyone is *not* doing it, and we can shine by comparison. So we must overcome the inertia keeping us from accomplishing what is admittedly a challenge but is also a simple fact of life on the road to self-improvement.

Presenting to an Audience of One

Recognize that you already spend 80 percent of your time communicating. You can learn to give a dazzling, persuasive presentation, so make a commitment. Ironically, those of us who depend on our communication skills the most are the last ones to admit we frequently give *presentations*. We may not recognize the one-on-one talk or a speech made to a small group as being a presentation. However, a speech is a presentation whether given to one or a hundred people.

When you decide to move forward with your goals to improve your performance, your life will change. When you adopt the principles in this book, you will be able to create organized, colorful, and memorable presentations filled with anecdotes and humor. You will be able to implement many of the sales and closing techniques that you have *learned* but have never quite made *work*. More importantly, you will have an improved level of success selling your ideas or your company's products. (I have seen many people complete my seminars only to wind up having significantly improved career opportunities.) You will be more motivated because you will feel as though you have control over the results of your efforts. In a sales presentation there are some things you can't change, but there are many things you can—if you learn how. Your arguments will be convincing, you will have better stories and anecdotes, and you will have more fun!

Building on Your Enthusiasm

If there is one thing that makes a great presentation it is passion—the heartfelt emotion that says to your listener, "I truly believe in what I am saying." This is the single most convincing tool you have at your disposal. Build on your enthusiasm. This emotion is contagious, and people who know how to communicate it are able to light fires under the rest of humankind. Think of the great communicators— John F. Kennedy, Dr. Martin Luther King, Ronald Reagan, Colin Powell.

You first should believe in everything you represent. It is the connection to the soul that makes this possible, and your stories, anecdotes, and personal experiences, with their humor and drama, provide the soul to your presentation.

The skills necessary to communicate passion and enthusiasm can be learned. The catch is that you have to feel it. Dale Carnegie once said, "Act enthusiastic, and you will feel enthusiastic." That may be so, but you also have to be true to yourself. You must believe in three things in order to be able to express enthusiasm with conviction: You must believe in your product, you must believe in your company, and you must believe in yourself. If one of those three things is missing, make a change and fix it. Get off the fence. Find out what it will take for you to become a believer in those three components, and then do as Dale Carnegie says—act enthusiastic! Later on, I will give you techniques and exercises for inspiring those listening to your presentation with the same explosive enthusiasm that you feel in your heart about your topic.

To be great, a presentation has to be unique. No one is going to get very excited if you sound as though you got your pitch out of a Chinese fortune cookie. A man working as a telephone solicitor once told me a woman on the line asked him point-blank if he was "a recording." Can you imagine how little enthusiasm he must have possessed to be asked if his voice was a recorded message?

It is very easy to develop a single presentation and deliver it day in and day out to all kinds of people. The individual who does so is playing a numbers game. There is something to be said for playing the numbers, but results from such an approach have distinguishing characteristics often associated with random action: They are unpredictable and can promote burnout.

Passion should be an integral part of the job of selling. When we are talking about working, the average adult today spends eight or more hours a day at his or her job. That is a lot of time. If you are going to do something anyway, why not do it with a little more enthusiasm? Charles Kingsley said it best when he pointed out that most people believe that comfort and luxury are the chief requirements for happiness in life, when all we truly need to be happy is something about which to be enthusiastic. This book attempts to get people fired up about their presentations. The more fun you have, the more people will be drawn to you, and the more rewards you will reap. My intent is for you to stop wasting energy, refine your presentation, and focus your efforts in a way that will produce the best results possible for a given prospect.

Knowing Your Audience

People sometimes ask me what the difference is between someone who closes a lot of sales and someone who just barely gets by, when both individuals appear similarly competent. I answer by saying it is generally a person's ability to analyze the audience and match a delivery style and content with the listeners' needs.

It helps to know your audience. Is it a group of teachers from Dubuque, or a team of biologists from the Department of Agriculture whose specialty is crop tolerance of salinity levels in river water? You have to know. In short, you have to do your homework. We will discuss the audience more thoroughly later in the book, but it is important to understand that to give a great presentation requires making the extra effort necessary to customize your talk and meet the needs of the individual or group who will hear it. It is an important part of making your presentation unique and memorable.

In order to have a persuasive presentation you will need to have completed some homework about your audience. You must be able to offer them a presentation customized to their needs, beliefs, and style. This takes preparation and requires doing the work necessary to find out something about your listeners beforehand. Unfortunately, this isn't always possible. When it isn't, you have to use your "standard" presentation found through experience to work most often on the majority of listeners.

Never Be Boring

When I have people present in front of a video camera during my training sessions, the first reaction they often have after seeing the playback is one of shock.

"Terri, I didn't realize how boring I sound!"

Yes, and sadly they are boring. Why? Typically because they have never listened to themselves speak while imagining what it would be like to sit in the audience. Would you like to listen to *you*? Would you be persuaded by *you*? Would you buy from *you*? Another reason people aren't interesting is they often think it doesn't matter if they are boring.

Some people assume because they work for a large company that the firm's name alone will sell the product. Some people believe (inaccurately) that their job is only to deliver brochures and answer questions. To be effective, they must do much more; they must be entertaining and worth listening to. *Never let a great product or a great company get in the way of a great presentation.*

Relying Too Much on Information

The number-one problem we find in working with sales professionals, however, is that their presentations rely on information rather than persuasion. A powerful sales presentation, by definition, is persuasive. If you haven't tried to make it persuasive, it probably isn't powerful.

Salespeople tend to think that if they give the client enough information, the sale will just fall in their laps. All presentations, however, have to be closed. If you don't get the order, you have wasted your time. If all you do is provide information, you are not likely to get a commitment from your prospect. The techniques in this book will allow you to give sales presentations that are persuasive.

Learning to Express Sincerity

You can also learn to communicate sincerity, a task that many people find difficult. This is not a book for slick operators who want to fool the public. This is a book for people who are sincere about what they are selling but could do a better job of getting their message across. We focus on those areas that you are able to control. We focus on your timing and organization. We build experience. We practice developing your skills during drills at home, before the actual presentation. You can learn to communicate more effectively.

Keeping Your Presentation Fresh

Whether or not we accept it, times change, economies change, and businesses change. Your presentation will constantly change and evolve based on the changing needs of your marketplace and your audience as well as what's happening in terms of the culture of the times. If you don't constantly monitor changes and adapt your presentation to the changing marketplace, you will miss opportunities. Whether or not we like it, if we fail to keep up with change, we tend to slide backward. The marketplace today is very different from that of the past, and the sales professional needs different strategies to compete successfully. Salespeople need polished, believable, and highly persuasive presentations if they expect clients in the coming decades to give them their business.

Such presentations are a component of the evolution of sales and are marked by the increased level of sophistication we find in the field of marketing in general which includes computer-generated graphics and sophisticated audiovisual presentations. The sales professional cannot sit on the sidelines and be overshadowed by the media he or she is using to display products. The sales professional must be the leader and focus of attention in any presentation. We will be discussing the use of laptop technology in presentations in Chapter 8.

Overcoming Bad Habits

I assume you already know something about selling. In order to learn the fine art of persuasive communications, however, you are going to have to acquire new skills. You will first have to overcome some bad habits—primarily how to stop providing too much information to people. You may also have to learn how to avoid hard-sell, manipulative closing tactics. If you can't look at your presentation and pull out the *so-what factors* (So what does it mean to me?), then odds are you are probably giving people too much information and not pulling out the action that you want them to take as a result of it.

Condensing Information to Save Time

Ben Franklin said that something is innovative if it is only 10 percent new. Today there are new ways to deliver a presentation that make it refreshing, innovative, and different. I feel one of the problems in sales training today may be overemphasis on and misinterpretation of two forms or approaches to selling—consultative selling and value-added selling. Consultative selling is a process whereby you act as a consultant while walking a person through the selling process. Value-added selling is offering additional features or services to your product in order to make it more desirable.

The problem is that many people think it means you have to put even more information into your presentation than you did previously. This and the ongoing information explosion, the Internet, and growing competition all are having a dramatic effect on the role of today's sales professional. As we enter a global, more diverse marketplace, the pressure from competition is only likely to increase. For the sales professional, the challenge is how to condense all this information and deliver it in a meaningful yet persuasive way to the listener.

Salespeople generally don't have time to educate clients for two or three hours on why they should do something. This book is designed to help you meet the challenge of how to take all the necessary material, refine it, and then present it so as to meet the very strict time parameters imposed by your client or decision maker. Suzette Haden Elgin, in her book, *The Gentle Art of Verbal Self-Defense at Work*, suggests that "no speech or presentation should ever last more than 20 minutes," because that is the average attention span of a listener. Of course there are a number of exceptions depending on the selling cycle and selling environment, but it is something to consider when you are building your next presentation.

The results of learning how to build a logical, persuasive sales presentation often include developing a sense of heightened self-esteem. Sales professionals will be able to discard any deceptive or manipulative tactics in favor of building logical persuasive arguments that move people toward action. The result is they generally feel more confident, empowered, and credible. They now can claim the role of someone who is advising and guiding a prospect toward making a decision.

Learning to Create a "Harm"

With honesty and integrity having become standards for the sales professional in the new millennium, the requirement to create a need in the mind of the prospect has become ever-more important. The sales professional needs new tools to help him or her become more persuasive. As consumers become increasingly sophisticated, salespeople need to create what we call "harms."

We will talk more about these techniques of persuasion in Chapter 3, but creating a harm means pointing out what undesirable consequence is likely to happen if the prospect does not buy your product or service or work with you. A harm has to be nonthreatening to avoid being manipulative. It has to be factual to conform to the standards of integrity that have been established. In the future, selling by using a harm will become a way to spur the client to action.

The Four Stages of Selling

Before we move into the specific techniques of persuasive presentations, let's establish the four basic elements that constitute a sale:

1. Attracting the prospect.
2. Interesting the prospect.
3. Convincing the prospect.
4. Closing the sale.

The progression of these elements is crucial. The important thing to remember is there are four distinct phases and each requires the prospect to undergo a change. If all we do is provide information, we fail to guide the client through the changes necessary to go from being just interested to taking action.

We address all of the techniques you will need to learn to take your clients from mere interest to closing the sale. *New Sales Speak* will be your guide in an exciting learning process that will produce unlimited benefits for you, your family, your employer, and your clients.

Sales Speak:
Selling, Speaking, and the Partnership Between the Two

What you can do, or dream you can do, begin it; boldness has genius, power, and magic in it.

—Johann van Goethe

There is an adaptation to a line from Shakespeare that says, All the world is a stage, and sales professionals play to the most discriminating audiences of all—their customers. What other group do you know that gets to pay for the performance after the show? Meanwhile, based on how you are speaking, your customers are deciding whether they even like you—a decision that could determine whether you get paid at all!

Everybody Sells Something

The process of living requires all individuals to sell at some point in their careers. We must sell ourselves to get our first job, entrepreneurs have to sell themselves to investors, CEOs sell their company strengths prior to an initial public offering, community residents sell their ideas to the city council. Teachers sell their students on the value of becoming educated and learning new material. A butcher persuades a customer to select a certain cut of choice meat. In each case, we are giving persuasive talks, though we may not be aware of it. For those of us who make our living in sales, nearly 75 percent of our time is spent communicating. Do we think of ourselves as public speakers? Certainly not! We would rather tame snakes than stand in front of our peers to give a presentation. Surveys show that public speaking is our single most feared activity.

Yet, how do we spend most of our days? In public speaking activities—we just don't like to think we do. We depend on our speaking skills to share our messages clearly and with credibility, whether we are speaking on the telephone, in a one-on-one meeting, or to a small group.

The Importance of Presentation Skills

Consider the following: Your public speaking and delivery skills are an immediate demonstration of executive ability within a company and may very well be the number-one reason why most business transactions are won or lost. In spite of that, people tend to minimize the importance of their presentation skills. Some will say, "Oh come on Terri, you know I've been speaking since I was in grade school— it's not that big a deal." Or they will say, "You know, I took a public speaking course when I was in college—I feel pretty good about it." Some people may even have had limited practice giving talks with their local business organization. While all these experiences are relevant and perfectly valid, what they don't do is take us to new heights.

The marketplace has changed, and, compared to the previous decade, the new millennium and beyond already are proving to be a new ballgame for the sales professional. It is a highly competitive market, and people are not apt to listen to sales presentations for entertainment. Decision makers are shopping harder than ever. You can bet they are checking up to five different suppliers before they make a decision. What they may actually be shopping for, however, is the right salesperson making the best case. What they often are looking for more than for the lowest price is the best overall package, whether that package is you, a product, service, philosophy, or idea.

Only a salesperson can lead them into making an informed decision. The salesperson who has the most charismatic and believable presentation, the best argument supported by the strongest facts, is the one who will be perceived as offering the greatest value. People will spend more money to work with those they like and will reject working with those they don't like, regardless of cost.

Why Is Giving Out Information Appealing?

It is the perception of value that counts. The client has to perceive your presentation as effective, your product or service as worthwhile. Just providing information makes you just like your competitor, and it doesn't mean that you are selling. There is no sense of urgency in an informative presentation. You may feel comfortable giving such an informative talk, but ask yourself, why? The reason you feel comfortable is because you never hear the word *no* when all you do is disseminate information.

Can We Learn to Speak Persuasively?

Persuasive public speaking is a learned activity. It is the application of formal principles of effective public speaking and debate strategy to the sales presentation. It is a new marriage between the strict principles found in the speech departments of our nation's college classrooms and the fascinating kaleidoscopic world of professional sales. It is a way to compete in the new millennium and to ensure ourselves of being on top of every element within our control, as we address our peers with ideas that need their decisions. It is the combination necessary to ensure our presentation has both excellent content and outstanding delivery. It is a way to make what we say credible and, most important, to make ourselves unique. We will address this subject specifically in Chapter 3.

Informal surveys that we have conducted show that anytime you undertake a prospecting call, you have approximately 30 seconds to make an impression. That's not much time. And whenever you give a one-on-one presentation, you generally have no more than five minutes to make a good impression. That's still very little time. Most of the time we are giving a presentation, people are determining whether or not they like us. It seems as though initially it has absolutely nothing to do with our professional knowledge.

I know we often choose to believe it's not true, but every day, people will make a decision whether they want to work with us based on our public speaking and presentation skills. Are we sharp? Are we articulate? Does our message draw them in? Do they feel compelled to listen to us as a result of that message? Or are they completely bored?

What Is the Three-to-Five-Company Rule?

When talking with a prospective client, you may safely assume yours is not the only game in town. For you to get to first base, the prospect must notice you and listen to what you have to say. For you to reach home plate, the client must perceive you and your product or service as outshining that of your competitor once the prospect has completed his or her value quest.

There definitely is competition out there—you know it, and so do your prospects. They will exploit it because competition works to their advantage. The serious prospect often will consider between three and five companies before making a final selection. We call this the *Three-to-Five-Company Rule*. If yours is the first presentation heard, the prospect may resist making a buying decision until having had enough time to scout the market. If yours is the last presentation, the prospect will compare every detail of what you say against what he or she has been told by all the other salespeople from different companies. In either case, your presentation will be critically evaluated. And so will you. I always try to determine if my prospective clients are working with someone else. If I can't tell, I assume that they are. Doing so forces me to be even more persuasive and competitive than I would be otherwise.

Is the Focus on You or Your Product?

People say to me, "Terri, I can 'walk the walk,' but how do I 'talk the talk'?" I always see that question as a sign that someone is on the right track to becoming part of the top 20 percent of producers. This individual realizes that the difference between being highly successful and merely average lies in his or her own actions and not with the product or company they represent.

Let me give you an example from the real estate industry. It illustrates the considerable weight a salesperson has in influencing a prospect's selection. Suppose you want to sell your house. Employing the Three-to-Five-Company Rule, you call several brokers to see who should get the listing. All are nationwide companies with referral services. Brokers from each company visit your house and describe their services to obtain your listing. Each asks for a 6 percent commission and offers to list your home in the Multiple Listing Service. An agent who sold your neighbor's house brought all the salespeople and brokers from his office through the house on a caravan. Naturally, you want the same thing. All three brokers assure you they will provide you with the identical service. Will they keep your house open Saturdays and Sundays, you ask? No problem.

The third broker leaves after finishing his presentation. You sit down and begin to figure out which company has the best program. What are the differences? You realize after struggling with the question, there are no differences! Each is identical. Each agent knew how to walk the walk and presented the features and benefits his or her company offers. There is one small difference, however. Each offer was made by a different person. So what are you going to do? Typically, you are going to pick the person you like the best. The person who you felt would work the hardest for you—and the person who built the best case. This happens over and over every day of the year. People pick the product based on who is selling it. People buy people. (If you haven't already done so, be sure to read Dale Carnegie's classic work, *How to Win Friends and Influence People*, which first addressed this topic.)

Your Presentation Reflects Who You Are

Now you say, "Well, Terri, I am what I am, and I can't change that. Either people like me or they don't." I am not advocating that you try to be someone you are not. You should always be true to yourself. People are going to like you based on what you say and do. In your role as a salesperson, that evaluation will be made based on your presentation. Do you want that presentation to sound lifeless, hesitant, and boring? Or do you want that presentation to sound enthusiastic, passionate, organized, and persuasive? When you are giving it, your presentation is you. It may be the only part of you that a prospect remembers—or forgets. Top sales professionals give memorable presentations. They not only know how to walk the walk, they know how to talk the talk.

If you are a sales professional, you understand that the selling process doesn't begin with your formal presentation. It starts much earlier when you are trying to get in the door of the prospective client. Knowing effective ways to explain how you can be of service to the company can get you a critical appointment with the manager.

Getting in the Door

I was working for the Achievement Group in 1987 representing professional speakers widely known for their ability to clearly communicate new and effective sales techniques. My job was to sell these speakers to corporate clients who needed to train and motivate their sales professionals.

The White Rose

My first territory included a large residential real estate organization. Headed by a man named Jim Emery, it was a highly successful group with nine offices, each having more than 50 agents. My goal was to deliver a group presentation to their sales staff. Management policy, however, prevented outside salespeople from giving presentations during staff meetings. The implied closed-door approach frustrated me, particularly for a sales organization, and it also stimulated my competitive imagination. I kept asking myself how I could possibly go around this barrier, but my colleagues were no help—they continued to discourage me.

When I asked other, more experienced sales professionals from the Achievement Group team what they would suggest I do, they responded: "Forget it, Terri, you will never get in there. It is a closed office. Move on to the next account." I questioned what the difference is between a closed office and an open office (I have never entered an office that was posted: "Open to vendors and solicitors—come on in!") The answer is, there is no difference, except for the amount of time and creativity it takes to get through the door!

There Is Only One Way In

I followed up anyway with phone calls and mailings, but nothing happened. I changed my strategy and began meeting with each manager separately, but every one of them said the same thing: If I wanted to get into the offices, I would have to have permission from Jim Emery. So I turned my attention toward getting an appointment with him. No such luck—he had a very good secretary, one who had been trained to screen calls from salespeople.

The more rejection I got, the more determined I became

to get inside their organization. I was beginning to realize just how difficult it was. I surmised that few, if any, training sales agents had given presentations to these people. If I could get inside, I knew it would be a great account.

Finding an Angle

The movie *Wall Street* gave me the inspiration I needed. In the movie, the lead character, played by Charlie Sheen, delivers a box of imported cigars to his prospect on his birthday. I decided I could come up with one of the "creative solutions" characterized in the film. I decided to buy a long-stemmed white rose and resolved to deliver it to Jim Emery in person. I felt a white rose was appropriate because it symbolized integrity (in addition to the fact that I was poor and my company didn't provide salespeople with expense accounts).

The only appropriate place that I could think to approach him was in the parking lot outside his office. So at 5:30 A.M. I took up sentry duty next to his parking stall, which was clearly marked with his name on it. After I had waited about an hour and a half, a car pulled up. The driver was obviously the man I had come to find. "Excuse me, are you Jim Emery?" I asked timidly, but somewhat reassured by the fact that I had on my best suit.

"Yes, I'm Jim. Who wants to know?"

"Just some young gal who needs about ten minutes of your time," I replied.

"What is she selling?" he asked, cutting to the chase.

"I don't suppose she is selling anything," I said, deferring the obvious. "I think she just needs to deliver this flower."

The laughter that crossed his lips was a great relief. He opened the card that I had included with my gift. It read: "Mr. Emery, please just give me ten minutes of your time. I definitely believe I have something that will be of interest to you."

"I don't have ten minutes," he said. "You have two minutes as we walk from this car to that door." Every debating technique I had learned in college sprang to readiness. I came up with more reasons in two minutes for why he would be at risk if he didn't meet with me than I had used in the last three months with all my other clients. My debate background and degree in speech communication paid off. I knew instinctively how to build my presentation and deliver it.

"Okay," he said. "I'll give you your ten minutes. Come back tomorrow at nine o'clock." I kept to his schedule and delivered my presentation in ten minutes. However, our meeting lasted one and a half hours. What exceeded my most exaggerated hopes was his sending a letter of recommendation to each of his managers telling them why they should let me make a presentation at their staff meeting. He was, by this time, convinced that it was essential for his agents to hear the story I had to tell. If they would adopt the sales posture I was promoting, he could be quite certain that his organization would be enriched.

Why Did It Work?

On another level, though, his cooperation came down to something more basic and more personal. I believe it was a direct result of my giving him the rose and doing so before anyone else was up and working that morning. It wasn't an expensive perk. It was just a simple thing that made him think that I believed he was special and that I was willing to be creative and work harder to earn his business. There is a big difference between buying business and earning business. Creative thinking can make a big difference in your gaining access to people. Once you have grabbed their attention, you can support your position by delivering a solid, professional persuasive presentation.

Getting in the door is the first part, but what you do after you get inside is equally important. This is where many people suffer from common shortcomings that adversely affect their results. The goal of this book is to provide you with the nine biggest sales presentation mistakes and show you how to avoid them so you can generate the best possible outcome for all your presentation opportunities.

When you become discouraged, I hope you will think of the white rose story, or one of the other stories I will share with you later in the book. I hope you will practice your public speaking skills with passion, and I hope you will develop the habit of presenting your ideas in a logical way formulated to generate action in what is unquestionably a competitive marketplace. Make a commitment! Miracles don't happen with an explosion and flash of light. They start out like a small snowball rolling downhill. Little changes become magnified over time. Today is the best time to start your personal journey toward what truly can be a miraculous future. To deliver dynamic presentations, we must learn to combine hustle with polish, persuasion, and uniqueness.

Applying the 80/20 Rule

Let's talk a little about what is near and dear to most of us—the bottom line. Whenever I begin to explain to people how important it is to them to enhance their presentation skills, someone always brings it up. They will say, "Okay. Let's just say that public speaking skills are as important as you say. How is that going to affect my bottom line?" And the simplest way for me to show you how it affects your bottom line is to get you to reflect on the *Pareto Principle*, also known as the *80/20 Rule*.

The Pareto Principle was developed by Vilfredo Pareto, an Italian economist. Pareto first identified the wealthiest people in England in order to determine what common denominators they shared. Ultimately, what he found was that the top 20 percent of the people in the country owned, controlled, or were responsible for 80 percent of the wealth. Through research and analysis, he began to realize that the distribution of wealth across populations is invariably unbalanced—but it is also mathematically predictable. He found that this imbalance was repeated consistently regardless of the time period or the country. The book, *The 80/20 Principle, The Secret to Success by Achieving More with Less*, by Richard Koch, provides an easy-to-understand overview of the Pareto Principle or 80/20 Rule. Koch, an entrepreneur and investor, is a strong advocate of the 80/20 Rule's being used by everyone in their daily lives. He suggests it can help individuals and groups achieve much more and enhance personal effectiveness and happiness, and it can multiply the profitability of corporations and organizations.

When researchers such as Koch began to confirm the truth in Pareto's findings, people began to use Pareto's theories measuring and predicting success in countless areas—not only in business and economics but in other areas where resources are allocated disproportionately. These might include people, goods, time, skills, and, yes—even sales. According to Koch, "Most studies find that the top 20 percent of salespeople generate between 70 and 80 percent of sales."

So, when you hear an irritated coworker complain, "Why is it that the top producers always get whatever they want?" it is because they are the ones who are bringing in the business and contributing most to the bottom line. It naturally follows that the people who bring in the business and generate revenues are the ones who have the most power, especially in a sales environment.

Since it is the top 20 percent of sales professionals who will generate more than three-fourths of the results in an organization, perhaps we should look more closely at the characteristics of this elite group of individuals. What is it that makes them so much more productive than the 80 percent who are attempting—but apparently failing—to achieve the same thing?

Dare to Dream

Those in training and development have always wanted to know: What is it that the top producers in the upper 20 percent are doing that the bottom 80 percent are not? And if there were something significantly different, can we pull it from the top 20 percent and insert it into the bottom 80 percent to make a difference where it counts? The answer is a resounding *yes*.

I am reminded of the movie, *Rudy*, about the life of Rudy Ruettiger, the Notre Dame football player who spent his entire college career hoping to play a single game. His final moment of glory serves as testament to the fact that Rudy fulfilled his boyhood dream. Although Rudy had few innate talents when it came to football (a fact of which he was reminded during grueling practice sessions) his heart and soul cried out to be among the famous Fighting Irish. Rudy played only one game, but he never quit the team, nor was he cut. He was tenacious and persistent. Many young people who get discouraged when they don't see enough action simply give up, but not Rudy. Today, because of his determination, he can truthfully say that he played football for Notre Dame.

Rudy is now a successful motivational speaker whom I have had the pleasure of meeting. For years Rudy wanted to make a movie about his kooky football record because he thought it would be inspirational to others. The response from Hollywood: "You must be kidding!" Once again he didn't give up but kept knocking on doors until one finally opened. Eventually, his dream of producing a movie came true. The best part is that the film received great reviews. Rudy Ruettiger's life is a success because he was willing to do what most other people will not do: Keep going when everyone else says, "Give up, it's hopeless—you're dreaming!" Remember never to let other people's limitations on you serve in place of your own goals.

Three Characteristics of Top Sales Professionals

In my opinion, there are three major characteristics that typify top sales professionals. They are (1) the psychological difference—all believe they can be top producers, (2) great listening skills—all are expert listeners, and (3) excellent presentation skills. If I were to list a fourth characteristic it would be a good sense of timing, the ability to be in the right place at the right time to spot opportunities. However, I also believe there is no such thing as luck. As the old saying goes, "Luck is when preparedness meets opportunity."

Psychological Difference

Let's take a look at the primary characteristic, one we know from our first class in sales—*the psychological difference.* I want you to know that I believe in the so-called psychological difference, and I think that everybody should have a psychological edge. In the early days of my selling career, I associated the psychological difference with being motivated. Before going to work I often would say to myself, "I need to get motivated. I need to get myself charged up. I need a little kick in the pants to really get me fired up for the day." Then I would think, "I know what I need to do, I need to get myself a couple of those motivational tapes!"

My first audiocassette program was by Dr. Denis Waitley, called *The Psychology of Winning.* It's a great audio package about making things happen and how to motivate yourself. And I thought, *Wow, this is just great.* Then I said, "You know, the other thing I am going to do is write down my positive affirmations. I'm going to put them on a card and I'm going to remind myself of what I need to do everyday." I kept telling myself that this was going to change me—this was what I needed.

I took out my 3×5 cards and I stuck them on my bathroom mirror where I could read them every day. And I would say while I put on my mascara, "I'm good! I can make this happen! Today is the best day of the rest of my life!" And I was really fired up. And I thought, "This will be the thing that will push me past the brink of success."

At the end of 30 days, I figured I had given it a pretty good test. Unfortunately, I may have left the house a slightly happier person, but it didn't really have any effect on my production. Needless to say, this wasn't the only factor that contributed to the psychological difference. I think the best way for me to explain what people really mean by psychological difference is to share with you the story of a colleague of mine. Mitch Gaylord is one of the people with whom I have the pleasure of working. You may be familiar with his name, which people associate with gymnastics. He was an Olympic gold medallist in gymnastics for the United States. Now Mitch works a lot with young people presenting programs on goal setting, motivation, and inspiration. A while back he called me on the phone and said, "Terri, I would really like to work with you for a bit before I go and have a videotape shot." I said, "Sure, no problem, Mitch." He came over and we were sitting across from each other and I was looking at him and thinking how impressed I was by his many accomplishments. So I asked him outright, "Mitch, what is it like to score a perfect 10 at the Olympics? I can't even imagine what it would feel like."

He said, "Terri, by the time you get to that final round, every single competitor who is on the floor is capable of scoring a perfect 10. It's not about who is capable, but who is going to pull it off at game time when the pressure is really on, and who will do it with the greatest consistency."

There's no question in my mind that every single one of you reading this is equally capable of scoring a perfect 10 presentation, but the question is how we can teach you to do it when the heat is really turned up at game time.

Denis Waitley addresses the psychological edge winners have in *believing* they can reach the ambitious goals they set for themselves. They *know* they can do it, so they try harder. If you think you can't do something, why waste your time even trying? Most people just compromise themselves by trying halfheartedly. That way, when they fail, they have an excuse for their poor performance. Besides, trying harder translates into more work. Here's a fact: People who are lazy rarely make it to the top. Successful people do the things unsuccessful people don't want to do.

The Power in Listening

The second factor that separates the top producer from the average or status quo is listening-communication skills. A colleague of mine once shared an insight about Donald Trump, a man known to be respected by his competitors and revered by his associates for, among other things, his ability to listen. Trump has an amazing talent for sitting down in a one-on-one discussion and asking probing questions that draw out material he uses later in arguments supporting his presentations. This is one of the key reasons why he is such an effective competitor.

I have many clients who come to my training programs because they are concerned about their speaking skills. They realize that if they can improve their presentations they will be more effective sales professionals. Almost no one, however, worries about their listening skills, at least not until they see themselves on videotape and realize they need help. You may have heard the quotation from writer Ambrose Bierce, who once said, "A bore is a person who talks when you wish him to listen." Listening is an active process that requires intense thought. We need to listen to our clients and prospects as well as to ourselves.

When we tape participants in a sales training role-play session, they often say, "Now I understand what the customer's question was!" The comment usually comes after they realize they didn't answer the prospect's question, or they responded with an answer that would send any rational person across the street into the waiting arms of the competition. Often we don't hear what our clients are saying, or we select an answer that is inappropriate because we really don't understand the question. Our mouths take charge after our brain shuts down. We just don't take the time to listen. If we slip into auto-pilot and respond mechanically, I guarantee it does not impress our audience.

There is a joke about a famous psychiatrist who is approached at a cocktail party by a solicitous guest. "My dear doctor," he begins. "How can you stand to listen to people's problems all day long? It must be dreadfully depressing." Somewhat taken aback by the man's provocative question, but determined not to be easily annoyed, the psychiatrist quips: "Listen? Who listens?"

Let Me *Forget About* What You Said

How many of you have ever worked with a client or prospect that said, "I'd like to think about it"? Let me explain what happens when they begin to "think about it." On average, prospects will retain only half of what we tell them. You may have delivered the most dazzling presentation of your life, but the moment you walk out the door your listeners will lose varying amounts of the information you just shared with them. In fact, within the first 10 minutes they will start to lose information. To begin with, they retained only 50 percent of what you told them. Within the first 10 minutes, they can lose up to 10 percent. By the time they go home, spend some time with their family, play with the kids, they can lose another 10 percent. The following day (barring any unforeseen crises like a speeding or parking ticket), they could lose another 10 percent. So by the time you make your follow-up call and say, "Hi, Mr. and Mrs. Jones, this is Terri Sjodin—I just wanted to follow up with you regarding the presentation I made the other day . . ." they may have already forgotten nearly three-fourths of everything you told them! So they say, "Oh my dear, we have been so busy, we haven't even had a chance to think about it." The entire time that we believed our prospects have been *thinking about* our proposal, in reality they have been literally *forgetting* about it!

The irony with respect to listening is while we may not do it very well, we spend lots of time trying. As business professionals, we spend nearly three-fourths of our working time communicating, and 40 percent of that is in listening, according to Madelyn Burley-Allen, author of *Listening: The Forgotten Skill*. The rest we divide between speaking, reading, and writing, with speaking representing about a third of our efforts. Reading represents about 15 percent and writing less than 10 percent of our time devoted to communicating. When more than a third of our entire working time is spent listening to others, doesn't it make sense we should examine our listening habits even before we polish our speaking skills?

Burley-Allen cites the example of a manager who was curious about the amount of time he spent just in listening so he asked his secretary to keep track of his time on the telephone just listening. He was shocked to find the company was paying him nearly 40 percent of his salary, or $18,000, for this function alone. However, on average, people are only about 25 percent effective as listeners. If the manager's listening skills were at only 25 percent efficiency, his employer would be paying him some $13,500 for time he spends listening ineffectively.

We can help improve our clients' retention by creating a presentation worth listening to and by improving our own listening skills. After all, listening as a method of taking in information is relied upon much more than reading and writing combined. We can help our prospects remember our presentation by influencing whether they understand it in the first place—a big factor in how much of it they remember. Improving our own listening skills also will help us overcome our prospects' objections and give us better control over the sales situation.

Are You Tuning Out Objections?

Imagine a situation in which the prospect is trying to wrest control of the sales call. Imagine yourself trying to maintain control to close the sale. Now think of yourself engaged in these activities: focusing the conversation on the points you want to make, listening to the client's comments, responding to them, presenting your argument—listening, responding, presenting.

Now imagine yourself in a similar situation with a difficult prospect, only instead of engaging the person, you are ignoring what they are saying, choosing instead to recite the list of features and benefits of your product. This is a situation more common than you might imagine; through videotape playback and workshop drills, we find that people frequently tune out their prospects' questions and also their objections. Burley-Allen calls this Level 2 listening— hearing the words but not really the deeper meanings of what is said.

In which of these two situations are you going to have the greatest chance for success? The first one, of course, because you are exercising control over the presentation and continuing to guide the prospect toward the best possible outcome. To some extent, every prospect is difficult, and every transaction requires expert listening skills to connect with the client and close the sale.

Three Dimensions to Listening

There are three dimensions to listening that account for how well we hear what the prospect says. The first is empathy, the second is information processing, and the third is critical listening.

Empathy

Empathy means that we listen from the heart. We avoid prejudging the prospect's statements. Have you heard the phrase, "buyers are liars"? It is a cynical comment you will want to ignore. The buyer may well employ counterfeit objections but also will have legitimate concerns. Your job is to decipher which of his or her stated concerns are bogus and which are real. To discount all the prospect's objections without determining the facts is to act without empathy. Listen for the buyer's true concerns. Be empathic.

Information Processing

The second dimension of listening is information processing. It means objectively collecting and categorizing facts from the prospect, then prioritizing what you hear. There are separate activities associated with information processing. To be an information processor you must:

1. Recognize the central idea.
2. Identify the main points.
3. Recall the details.
4. Summarize.
5. Draw references.
6. Ask insightful questions.

In my workshops, I usually ask salespeople, "What is the goal of your presentation?" They sometimes look at me as though they don't know what I'm talking about. "What do you mean?" they ask. Well, what is the point of your presentation? What do you want to happen as a result of this presentation to your clients? Do you really know what the single, overriding message is that you are trying to get across? If you aren't clear on what your central idea is, your prospective client isn't going to know either. You may have been working in your field for 20 years, you may have all the supporting figures in your head to prove a long string of claims, but if you can't share your message in a way that makes people understand the main points, you will be spinning your wheels.

If your clients cannot recognize the central idea of your message, if they cannot identify the main points, recall important details, summarize the information, and ask insightful questions, then you have to wonder, "How effective was I?" Try putting yourself in the role of one of your clients and see if you can apply the above criteria to your presentation. Then try it on feedback from your next customer. Be aware of yourself as a deliverer of information.

Critical Listening

A listener will critically evaluate your presentation, including every claim in it, whether you pay attention to what you are saying or whether you put your mouth on automatic and flip the "on" switch. What happens, though, when your prospect asks a question? Are you going to respond in a way that reinforces your message and continues moving him or her toward the close? Or are you going to confuse the prospect with a response that isn't really related to the question asked? Remember, the customer is testing your credibility. Are both you and what you say believable? In order to use the excellent opportunity a question offers, you will need to develop and employ critical listening skills. Remember that your prospects will be listening to you from a critical standpoint as well.

Effective listening not only involves paying attention to others—it involves tuning in to ourselves. If you heard your own presentation and you wanted to evaluate it for credibility, how would you do it? Here are the five keys to assessing the third listening dimension, critical listening:

1. Recall the main claims.
2. Identify the premise.
3. Evaluate the evidence.
4. Be objective, not defensive.
5. Ask how credible is the speaker.

Since your listeners will critically evaluate your presentation by performing these steps, doesn't it make sense for you to do the same evaluation of your presentation before delivering it? I am reminded of a question by Hal Becker in his book, *Can I Have Five Minutes of Your Time?*, in which he asks readers, "Did you ever talk yourself out of a sale? Did you go on and on until it was too late? Did you ever LISTEN yourself out of a sale? NEVER!"

In practice, many of your prospects will not be good critical listeners. They will jump to conclusions based on personal experiences that may have little or nothing to do with what you have been telling them. If you are a good critical listener, you can recognize these misinterpretations when the prospect poses a question. You will be applying your critical listening skills to the feedback you get.

The important thing is for your prospect to hear the right message and not make a decision based on incorrect assumptions. It is crucial, therefore, to be objective in evaluating your client's questions and comments. You can clarify and reinforce your points on the way to guiding the prospect toward the close.

Persuasive Presentation Skills

The third factor that separates the top producer from the average person is persuasive presentation skills. Top producers have a phenomenal delivery. There's something about them that is charismatic—people say it is the person's polish. But polish comes from practice, and charisma comes from certainty. It's owning the material in your mind, spirit, and presence.

The Absence of Dazzling, Persuasive Presentation Skills

To appreciate just how important public speaking skills are today, think of the 1992 presidential election in which Independent Ross Perot attracted a large number of voters who were disillusioned with the two traditional parties. In spite of his independent status, Perot posed an intriguing challenge to both incumbent Republican President George Bush and Democratic candidate Bill Clinton. A factor in the campaign, however, was a series of debates between the leading candidates and another involving their vice-presidential running-mates. Unfortunately for Perot, his selection for vice president was not a dazzling public speaker.

Vice Admiral James Stockdale is a highly respected Vietnam War hero and an accomplished military executive. But he is not a strong presenter. Viewers who saw the debates will never forget the point at which Stockdale began fiddling with his hearing aid, stopping the talks dead and creating the impression, albeit erroneous, that he may be too old to run for the nation's second-highest office. Polls taken afterward showed that imperfections in Stockdale's style and delivery gave undecided voters the reason they needed to discount the Perot ticket altogether. Instead they moved on to the task of deciding between the two major candidates. If Stockdale had possessed the public speaking skills of Colin Powell or Ronald Reagan, is it possible the outcome of the election would have been altogether different?

The interesting thing to remember is that Stockdale's sterling qualifications earned him a *chance* at high office, but they were not the deciding factor. He had to demonstrate in person to voters that he was qualified and convince them they would be making the right choice if they relied on him and his running-mate.

We might think of the debates as a sort of national public job interview. That idea suggests to me that any job applicant who thinks a resume alone, without benefit of a convincing oral presentation, will secure a corporate position is apt to be looking for work for quite some time.

Everyone Remembers a Great Speaker

Everybody loves to hear great speakers. What is more important is that we remember them. When we think of great presenters we think of Dr. Martin Luther King Jr., John F. Kennedy, and Ronald Reagan—all were considered great speakers and communicators. When they spoke they used no visual aids, no handouts, no brochures. They were just individual men standing before thousands of people and able to move the masses on what often were perceived as unpopular issues. But they did it—how? Through the art of the delivery. You always remember the great speaker, even if the individual is not such an admirable person. Take Stalin, for example. Or even two-term president Bill Clinton. In all honesty, if Clinton had had the public speaking skills of Stockdale when he was going through his problems with Monica Lewinsky, does anyone really think he would have survived his second term?

But we are moved as a country by the individual with great delivery. Also, we often tend to remember another type of presentation—the poor presentation. Yet whom do we forget? It's the average speaker, the one who is just fair. Remember that if you look back on your presentation and think it was just okay, or it was fine, then you may have just delivered the most forgettable presentation possible. That's why every single presentation that you deliver has to be the best one you have inside you.

Among all the people who may read this book, I have one particular reader in mind: the goal-setter who wants to be the best salesperson possible. My compliments go to you for wanting to achieve a level of personal fulfillment through attaining excellence. Striving to become a great salesperson means aiming to be a great public speaker and presenter. Achieving that takes having a psychological difference, sharp listening skills, and the ability to give a persuasive presentation.

Overview

- Everybody sells something, whether it is a product, a service, a philosophy, an idea, or even oneself on a job interview.
- Training in public speaking and advanced presentation skills is an important component in self-development and will also help ensure greater success within a selling environment.
- The Three-to-Five-Company rule reminds us that we constantly must be aware that most buyers or decision makers will consider between three and five competitors during the same period that they are considering us.
- People buy people, and your presentation reflects who you are.
- Tenacity, creativity, time, and perseverance—combined with a dazzling presentation—spell "fierce competitor" in today's market.
- There is a big difference between earning business and buying business.
- The three simple characteristics of top producers are (1) the psychological difference, (2) great listening skills, and (3) excellent presentation skills.
- We always remember a great speaker, but we also remember someone else—the terrible speaker. Who are we most likely to forget? The person who gives an average presentation—the one that was *just fine*.

Next: Now that we have given you a general overview of how important it is to develop strong presentation skills, in the next chapter we will look at one of the most common mistakes people make in giving a talk—*winging it*.

Mistake Number 1:
Winging It

The concept of "I'll play it by ear" is a guarantee of mediocrity at best.

—David A. Peoples, author, *Presentations Plus*

One of the most common problems people face in delivering a good presentation is that instead of preparing diligently as they might, they just forge out in front of an audience and hope for the best. They simply wing it. If you are a talented, experienced speaker, you might get away with this. However, most people typically perform poorly, and others often notice.

When you wing it, your presentation usually hops around all over the place, and your listeners are jerked around with it. The story line doesn't pretend to exhibit a logical, progressive flow. It makes it very difficult for a listener to follow where you are going, and most of the time people leave out half the points they want to cover, including the close.

People say, "I know my print material pretty well—I'm going out there, and I'm just going to wing it. Whatever comes out will be good enough."

This is a fundamentally bad idea. I must admit we sometimes find ourselves actually admiring the unfortunate individual who is giving such a spontaneous presentation only because we can't help but think how courageous they are to get up in front of a group with so little preparation! However, when you wing it, you're presentation typically is a terrible waste of your time, not to mention your clients' time—time that could have been used more effectively.

To pay so little attention to the delivery of a presentation is to say, in effect, it doesn't matter whether you do a good job. This attitude reflects a kind of denial that frequently is fueled by ignorance of the impact your words can have on your overall success. Allow me to share a story that explains why making this kind of investment in your presentation is worthwhile, even when you may not think so.

Never Underestimate the Power of Your Presentation

A client of mine was asked to speak at a public meeting in support of a local political candidate. Citizens were attempting to rout incumbents from an elected board, and the new office-seeker provided fresh ideas. Reluctantly, my client agreed to the public speaking challenge because he felt it was the right thing to do. Besides, his wife already had accepted the invitation on his behalf. For the purpose of this story, I will call my client Bob.

When he called me, Bob was terrified at the prospect of addressing a large audience. He had little experience and less self-confidence. I got his desperate plea on a Friday.

"Terri, I don't know what I'm going to do," he said. "I

have to make a presentation in front of several hundred people at a political rally next week. Can you help me?"

I said, "Sure, Bob. No problem." We began work on his talk by creating an outline. We established the main points he would make, developed the supporting material, and wrote in the stories and anecdotes. We worked on the talk all weekend. By the meeting Monday night, Bob was about as ready as he was going to be. If you have ever been to a heated public gathering, you can appreciate how intimidating it can get. This was no office staff meeting where people are paid to sit quietly and pay attention. This was an emotion-packed gathering of concerned citizens.

Whew! It's Over

Bob walked into the large auditorium and strolled to the podium. His knees were shaking, but the average person couldn't tell he was scared. No matter how nervous he was, we both knew he could do it. As he began his talk, it became clear his speech had a framework. It was logical, it adhered to the proper formula, and it had a specific objective he wanted to fulfill. It had impact, it was memorable—and it worked. The audience rose to their feet, clapped, cheered, and whistled. He was a star with a smash hit. His first thought, however, was not what a great job he had done. It was "Whew, it's over!" Except it wasn't over. There was someone in the audience Bob hadn't noticed. Bob's vice-president, three management levels above him, was among the attendees.

New Position Opens

"Bob, I had absolutely no idea," the executive began. "You are a powerful speaker. I want to talk to you about a position we have coming up that requires someone with your skills. If you are free tomorrow about nine o'clock, stop by my office so we can discuss it."

Not only did Bob do well during the interview, suddenly

he found himself within the executive inner circle. With his position, he received a substantial raise, bonus structure, and car allowance. That isn't bad for a free talk. The story has a happy ending, but what if Bob had declined the speaking engagement? He would have missed a great opportunity for self-improvement. Or what if Bob hadn't practiced and prepared? As it was, Bob's sphere of influence and his position, not to mention his income, were enhanced. Though Bob was extremely anxious about the task, he attempted it anyway, and succeeded!

Had Bob winged his talk, as many people do, it would not have had nearly the same impact. With a lackluster performance, he probably wouldn't have been approached about the job opening. It is important to put passion into every presentation and to do adequate advance planning in order to create opportunities. You may think you are talking to someone of limited means and authority. However, little fish have a habit of traveling with big fish.

How to Avoid Winging It

In order to fix the chronically common problem of winging it, we must start at the beginning with our attitude. First, we need to stop thinking of the presentation arena as a kind of bullfight with us playing the role of a matador. See yourself more as a symphony conductor who needs to practice before a concert. The first thing I want you to consider is your format. There are four different speaking formats:

1. *Impromptu*—speaking without physical prompts, but using a simple mental outline to speak in the moment.
2. *Extemporaneous*—speaking with the aid of a written outline.
3. *Manuscript*—a presentation delivered word for word from a written document.
4. *Memorized*—the presentation is rehearsed but recited from memory.

Selecting the appropriate format for your talk is the first step in addressing the problem of winging it. If we know what format we want to use, we have some idea of how to begin our preparation. That's right, *preparation*—the word is synonymous with *time*. If you want to give a good presentation, you will have to spend time preparing it.

Thorough Preparation

No matter which format you choose, remember to keep track of where you are headed with your argument. People ask me whether it really is necessary to do this much work before giving a talk. I know from experience even extremely talented people generally do not cover everything unless they list all the issues on paper first, then study them. When you wing it, you tend to leave out important ideas or stray off course. People spend too much time on issues that don't deserve it, while more important points get underemphasized. Let's take a detailed look at the four major presentation formats.

Impromptu

Impromptu means that you are speaking from a mental outline and you have already formulated what you want to cover. Giving an impromptu talk provides great freedom to interact with the audience and, if done well, can show how knowledgeable you are about your subject. Yet giving an impromptu talk has distinct disadvantages when you are trying to be persuasive. Recalling and selecting just the right words to describe what you are talking about can be a challenge for many people when giving impromptu talks. Someone giving an impromptu talk might be mistaken by the audience for someone who is winging it, but the two are quite different in that the former requires preparation.

Extemporaneous

An extemporaneous presentation is one you prepare in advance and deliver from an outline. The presentation is not written out word for word. The most common format for the sales professional, and the one we selected for Bob's talk, it allows the presenter to adjust his or her presentation as questions arise.

Extemporaneous means you are speaking from a physical outline, usually just a single page or two. You present from an outline, a copy of which can easily be handed to your clients whom you are addressing. I strongly recommend most people employ the extemporaneous format when speaking to clients and customers. Why? There are several reasons.

When you have the outline in front of you, I can guarantee that you will never walk out the door saying to yourself, "Oh, my gosh—I forgot to cover something!" You can always refer to the outline, and it will keep you on track.

The second thing is that when the people to whom you are speaking or giving a presentation have an outline in front of them, it will keep them on course with what you are saying. And the pleasing fact about it is that they will undoubtedly take notes on it during your presentation. And despite all your work preparing glamorous brochures and media kits, your single outline handout on a lone sheet of paper will become the most significant presentation piece in your publications package. Why? Because this is the handout your listeners now own. (They own it because they put their notes on it.) And we always hold on to the one thing for which we feel ownership. That's why you really need to use a one-sided, single-sheet outline during your presentation. It keeps your listeners involved and absorbed, and better yet, it helps them to retain greater amounts of information from your presentation.

Drawbacks of this format include the possibility of forgetting words necessary to nail down arguments precisely. If you have ever stumbled during a presentation while trying to find the right word, you understand the problem. The presentation can also become lopsided if the speaker spends too much time on the beginning and rushes through the second half to meet time constraints.

Manuscript

In a manuscript format, the entire presentation is written out word for word. Speakers then read every word of a manuscript presentation. They know what will be said is exactly what is intended. The speaker knows the language will remain vivid and compelling and the presentation will stay within fixed time limits. A manuscript is often used to deliver important messages, say by a government spokesman or at a scientific seminar.

Disadvantages include the likelihood the discourse will sound like an essay since people rarely write the way they speak. The talk may also sound stiff. The style makes it difficult to react spontaneously to the listener or audience. It requires a great deal of preparation to make it sound professional and not canned.

Memorized

A memorized presentation is written in manuscript form and committed to memory. This format was very popular in years past. Today, most salespeople prefer the extemporaneous style. I personally appreciate the memorized format because it allows the salesperson to focus on his or her audience. It is particularly effective in formal presentations. However, it requires extensive practice and commitment in order to be employed effectively because, if your mind goes blank . . . need I say more?

One effective exercise we do in our training sessions is to videotape sales professionals responding to objections they have written out and placed in a hat. When they realize these objections repeatedly occur, they see how much more persuasive they could be if only they practiced and memorized the responses ahead of time.

Having your presentation and answers to questions memorized in advance is useful, particularly since a prospective client may allow you only a few minutes. Even better is including the answers to your most commonly asked questions right in your presentation.

When I was working for the Resource Dynamics, I was teamed with a salesperson named Colette. She had come from an entirely different kind of company, and although she was familiar with the training industry, she didn't know how to overcome the objections she was getting over the telephone with our product. So she would listen to me on the phone and was impressed by the way I handled objections. She wondered how she could incorporate my techniques into her routine. Though it helped to listen to me, she didn't have ready access to the many responses needed to overcome all the varied questions and objections.

The way we solved this was to audiotape my presentation and record my responses to questions and prospects' objections. We did this over a number of calls, then had the tape transcribed. We later took the transcription, edited it, and posted it on the wall. That way, she could sit at her desk, make her calls, and if the prospect gave her an objection, she could look right up to the appropriate response. She had about eight objections with their responses right underneath them, all set in large type. After awhile, the responses became ingrained, and she was able to take down the written responses from the wall. But it really helped her to record what I was saying, transcribe it, and put it right in front of her desk where she made her phone calls. It just reinforces the point that having your presentation and/or your answers to questions memorized in advance can be very useful, particularly when you have little time and want a fast comeback. Employing memorization to handling objections is a very appropriate use of this format.

How to Determine Which Format to Use

A lot of work goes into a good presentation. This is particularly true when you want to tailor your talk to each individual audience or prospect. You may have a single talk for several audiences, but it will be more effective if you take the time to customize portions of it to meet the needs of the specific group you are addressing.

Here are some general guidelines in determining your format and putting together your presentation:

- Consider the time allotted for your talk (we will discuss this in more detail later in Chapter 4 and several of the other points in later chapters).
- Take the time to prepare and practice using a logical outline.
- Be sure to cover all points needed to communicate your message.
- Be sure that your presentation covers each of the points clearly and consistently.
- Make a determination whether you will be addressing a small or large audience.
- Select visuals appropriate to your audience.
- Give a copy of your outline to your audience.

Advantages of a Logical, Persuasive Presentation

You have the opportunity as a professional to deliver sharp, inspiring, memorable presentations. Or you can deliver limp, lifeless talks that don't persuade anyone to do anything except, perhaps, promise to call you later. One type of presentation makes things happen, the other doesn't. The choice is up to you. A tight presentation has good flow and keeps the audience's attention, it covers all the points you intended to make, and it meets your parameters for time as well as meets the needs of your audience; it has high impact.

What About No Time to Prepare?

People might ask, "Well Terri, what if I simply don't have the time necessary to put together an effective presentation?" The secret lies in careful planning of what you want to say. In Chapter 4, we include a sample presentation outline that will help you put together an overnight presentation, which should be adequate for many situations. The important thing is for you to review your facts and source materials and follow your written outline.

Overview

- Mistake Number 1 is winging it. When you wing it, it is often a terrible waste of quality presentation time.
- Never underestimate the power of your presentation. You must prepare and rehearse as much as possible.
- The four types of speaking formats are (1) impromptu, (2) extemporaneous, (3) manuscript, and (4) memorized.
- In a selling environment, I suggest using the extemporaneous format in which you speak from an outline.
- In the case of the overnight, or last-minute presentation, use the extemporaneous format outline found in Chapter 4.

Next: We have looked at one of the most common mistakes people make in creating a presentation—winging it—and the various ways to avoid it. We will turn our attention in the next chapter to another very common problem—being overly informative rather than persuasive.

Mistake Number 2:
Being Too Informative versus Persuasive

Our danger is not too few, but too many options . . . to be puzzled by innumerable alternatives.
—Sir Richard Livingston

Why This Is the Biggest Mistake

This chapter encompasses the biggest mistake made by most sales professionals in the field today. This mistake is so common that it is literally costing companies millions of dollars every year. The mistake we are making is that our presentations have become too informative rather than persuasive.

If you find you are meeting with a large number of clients, but are completing few transactions, one question you should ask yourself is, "Have my presentations become too informative versus persuasive?" Let's face it, it's far more comfortable to dispense information than it is to persuade someone to act. Selling can be challenging. But it is a mistake to think that the way to improve your closing ratio is to dump so much information on a client that the person feels guilty enough to do business with you.

The unfortunate truth is that people will suck you dry for information and then use all that information to negotiate another deal somewhere else. What we don't want to think about is that while we are being philanthropists communicating all this information, we can be hurting more than we are helping ourselves.

Define Your Role

There are different ways to deliver a presentation, but the one we need to master is that of persuasion. When I urge you to be persuasive, you might start to get defensive. You could say, "Terri, that's just not me—I'm not like that," or "I don't know how to do that—I don't have that kind of personality." You have to define what your role is when you are selling, and you have to decide just what it is you want to have happen as a result of your presentation. If you are selling a product, service, idea, philosophy, or even yourself, you generally want some type of action. This alone means that you are trying to be persuasive, not informative.

As a salesperson, you are never strictly an informative speaker. There is intent tied to your message. You may pull back from this suggestion and say, "Oh, I don't want to do that—I don't want to be a hard-sell closer." "I won't be that aggressive with my clients." You might even secretly think, "I just don't want to be in sales," or if you are in sales, "I don't want to be perceived as that kind of person." Let me assure you I am not trying to turn you into a personality you are not. In order to deliver a persuasive presentation, you don't need a certain kind of personality, all you need is to have one—and everyone does. You merely need to learn how to express it. Your personality and the intent of your message are two different things.

Three Presentation Styles

The first thing you should note is there are only three types of presentations that anyone can deliver—informative, persuasive, and ceremonial. The two main differences between a persuasive talk and either a ceremonial or informative one are that the persuasive talk begins by building an argument and concludes with a call to action (the close). A persuasive presentation is one that leads the listener toward doing something specific—usually signing the contract or setting up your next appointment.

Ceremonial speeches appeal to the values cherished by everyone present. The speaker tries to create a type of communion with the audience. Award ceremonies, acceptance, after-dinner, welcome, and farewell speeches all fall into this category.

Informative speeches are the most common and the most common trap for salespeople. When they should be delivering a persuasive talk, they give an informative one instead. The informative speech or presentation should not be the salesperson's tool of choice, although you would never know it by how many people use it. If you were to survey sales organizations across the country and ask individuals what kind of presenter they were among the three categories, they would typically say informative. But under no circumstances should you ever, when you are selling, be an informative presenter.

Informative presentations are intended to be objective. They promote audience understanding, foster cooperation, and present the subject matter in an unbiased way. The whole point is to promote learning. As a salesperson, do you want to educate your customer, or do you want to sell him something? The first responsibility of an informative presenter is to be unbiased. An informative presenter is supposed to tell all sides of the story. So, unless you are going out into the field and bringing all your competitors' materials with you saying: "Here is my material, and here are all the materials from my competition so you can make a decision," you are not an informative presenter. Why? Because an informative presenter is supposed to be unbiased, tell both sides of the story, be cooperative versus competitive, and promote learning. Is there a group of individuals whose job it is to be informative? Of course there is: teachers.

I frequently hear people say, "But Terri, aren't the best presentations a combination of both information and persuasion?" Yes, sometimes we want to inform and persuade, but too often we accomplish only one objective— the wrong one. In the last 10 years, with all the student training videotapes I have watched, I have *never* looked at a single one and said, "You know what? Your presentation is far too persuasive, we need to put in more information." It's never happened. Why? Because that's not the problem. It's easy giving information—there's no risk. We don't hear the word "no." There's no pain, anxiety, or fear associated with information. Somewhere along the line people started thinking, "Maybe if I give my prospects enough information, my products and services will sell themselves." In a perfect world, maybe that would happen. But it rarely does. In order for people to take action, you have to build a strong, persuasive case explaining why they should take action, specifically with you.

Lingering in the Information Zone

Many professionals have a tendency to linger in the *information zone* citing features and benefits and delay getting into the *persuasive zone*. Either they are not persuasive enough, or they save the persuasive material until the very end when it's often too late. The customer has little incentive to make a buying decision following a predominantly informative presentation. There is no sense of urgency to an informative presentation. At the end, the client may say, "Great, thanks for your information!" Meanwhile, they, or you, walk out the door. You hope they will return later and give you their business even if out of guilt more than for any other reason. I have news for you. Customers who don't buy don't feel guilty. Granted, it's comforting to know you won't hear the word "no" in this information zone, but you won't hear "yes" either.

Just for practice, try repeating the following phrase out loud: "As a sales professional, I am not an informative presenter."

Right, as a sales professional, you are not an informative speaker. You are a persuasive speaker.

And now, try repeating this: "As a sales professional, I am a persuasive presenter."

Fine; just keep repeating that to yourself.

Selling for The Achievement Group

My realization that we must do far more than merely offer information, including features and benefits, and instead structure the sales presentation persuasively comes from personal experience. I was fortunate in high school to have had speech coach Jim Caforio, who groomed a few of us from the time we were sophomores to be extremely competitive in speech and debate. By college, I was ahead of the pack in preparing formal presentations. By my junior year in college, I was ranked thirteenth in the nation for persuasive speaking, and during my senior year I was ranked sixth. That sounded impressive until I tried to begin to figure out what I was going to do when I graduated.

Because I was uncertain about my goals, I gathered my transcripts and other academic materials and went to meet with my career counselor. I spread out my files on her desk and said, "So, what do you think I should be?"

"Well, Terri, I would have to say that, with all your speech and debate background, I think you really should go into sales."

And I went, "Huh? You have to be kidding! I got a college degree so I wouldn't have to go into sales." (Did you ever think this way?) I was one of perhaps many people who mistakenly believed that if I had a college degree, I would be spared the sentence of having to earn a living by selling. I realize now the notion is ridiculous because everybody sells something. But, I always thought that I never wanted to be in sales.

"There must be some alternative!" I pleaded.

"Well, you know you could always go to law school," she said.

"That sounds so much better!" I exclaimed.

Mentally, I was all set to go to law school and started filling out the necessary applications. In the meantime, I accepted an internship with the office of then–U.S. Senator Pete Wilson (R-Calif.). Soon I started to figure out how much money I would need for three years of law school. At that time it totaled over $60,000. So, I merrily took my tuition estimate to my parents and they merrily returned it to me saying that I was on my own.

I thought, "Okay, how am I going to fund this academic adventure in such a short period of time?" Well, there was only one way that I knew of and that was in straight commission sales. So, I took a position working with a company called The Achievement Group. The firm set up marketing and promotion for a variety of national sales trainers. My job was to be a road warrior. We were given a stack of brochures and flown to metropolitan areas like Buffalo, New York. We lived there for the next six to eight weeks and encouraged people from different companies to attend large training and development seminars.

The position was strictly commission, so if you didn't sell anything you could go broke. The training consisted of learning the traditional selling program content—features and benefits, value-added selling, and consultative selling—to encourage people to attend the seminars.

So I went into the field loaded with brochures, my features and benefits presentation, my motivational tapes, and a lot of enthusiasm. After 35 days, I was starving to death. When you are working a straight commission job you are burning your own gas, paying for your own phones, and of course consuming your own time. After 30 days, if you are not selling anything, you are not happy!

Going Back to Basics

I was depressed, thinking to myself how much time I had wasted, and I needed a lift. So to make myself feel better, I decide to revisit a world where I had been successful—my college debate team. I decided to go over to the campus, drop in on my debate coach, and talk to her about old times. Maybe I would come back with renewed enthusiasm.

I walked into my coach's office, and she says, "Oh, my goodness—Terri Sjodin, an alumnus come back to visit us." Suddenly I began to feel better, and she says, "Well, do you want to sit down and judge a few speeches?" They were getting ready for a tournament.

"Sure, no problem," I offered.

"So, how are you doing out there in the real world?" she asks.

"Oh, it's great," I answer.

And she asks, "How are you enjoying sales?"

"Selling sucks. I hate it. I am so bad at it."

"I'm surprised to hear you say that," she says.

"Oh, why?" I ask.

"Well, I would think that with your debate background you would do very well."

"Oh, yeah—if they were the same thing. But they are two totally different things," I say.

"Really?" she asks, surprised.

"Oh, yes; it's all features and benefits. Then we do this consultative probing thing, and then we incorporate the value-added services. It's really very different."

"Really, I would like to see that," she says.

"Sure, I'll have to show you some day," I say.

"Well, how about right now?" she asks.

So we sat down and she does something that I always used to hate: she takes out an audiotape and slips it into her tape machine and presses the record button. Meanwhile, I go through my presentation. When I'm finished, she hits stop, ejects the tape, and tosses it over to me.

"So, do you really think you could win a debate round with that?" she asks.

"No," I explain. "That's the point. They are two totally different things."

"No, they're not." She says emphatically. "If you go home and really listen to this tape, I think that you're going to discover what the real problem is." Irritated, I make an attempt at a polite exit and walk out of her office, all the while thinking, "What does she know? She's an academic. Those who can, do, and those who can't, teach! This is the real world, and it doesn't work the same way it does in academia."

So, I was frustrated, but I figured, what the heck: I'll pop the tape into my car stereo and try listening to it through the ears of a debater. After hearing it, I decided to go home and revamp my entire presentation, just as I would a debate case. Essentially, I threw a lot of information out the window. In the process of evaluating my presentation, I finally realized what the difference is between a persuasive presentation and one that merely stresses features and benefits.

A feature is what something *is*, and a benefit is what it *does*. There is no sense of urgency in a features-and-benefits presentation. Inherently, it is an informative style. When you are giving an informative presentation, at the close, you are basically inviting your clients to say: "That's nice; now I want time to think about it."

I finally decided my coach was right about my presentation, and after making the necessary changes in it, I felt more confident about being persuasive and about delivering a persuasive case. As a result, my closing ratio increased significantly, and soon I became a top producer with The Achievement Group.

Being Persuasive Throughout Your Presentation

In developing a persuasive presentation, you want to create one that is persuasive throughout, not just toward the end. Although the persuasive ending is actually more common, it is far preferable to be persuasive throughout your presentation. For one thing, it puts less pressure on you as you approach the close, which makes the close easier. It also puts less pressure on your customer because you build your case throughout your talk as you lead him or her toward a decision.

Your focus should be on influencing the buyer's perception of what should be thought or done. You achieve this through careful management of your supporting material. I will show you how to do this later. Meanwhile, keep in mind that your intent is to sell the listener your product, service, or idea. If that doesn't happen, your efforts to provide him or her with information have been at your own—or your employer's—expense.

I'm not suggesting you eliminate the entire discussion of features and benefits. But I am going to ask you to adopt one simple concept from the field of debate—be more proactive than reactive. Debate would have us do one thing before we walk out the door with our list of features and benefits, or value-added services, and before we prequalify our clients. We would have to identify our 10 best arguments for why our clients should work with us, why they should work with our company, and why they should do it now. You would create your most persuasive argument at the beginning and put features and benefits at the end. This is how you develop a case that is balanced. Let me give you a simple example of why it is a good idea to put your arguments in the front and have your features and benefits at the end. If you think of a courtroom, the judge is at the front, the jury is off to the side, and there is a prosecuting attorney and a defense attorney. When the gavel hits the desk, and the trial opens, the attorneys stand up and begin with opening *arguments*. They don't begin with opening features and benefits. Next introduce all the evidence—testimony, witnesses, and so on—and provide the court with the arguments that were previously established at the beginning of the case. And when their presentation of the evidence and testimony is over, they end with what? Closing *arguments*! It's persuasive as well as informative, and that's where the balance is. And if you start to think of your presentation as a courtroom case where you are presenting arguments, I believe you will find a greater balance between persuasion and information in the body of your presentation.

Five Characteristics of a Persuasive Presentation

Persuasive presentations are intended to influence the perception of what should be thought or done. Intent is directly tied to the message. When we talk about influencing perception, we mean using language to influence a person's beliefs. Listeners must be able to relate information you provide to their individual situations and see themselves benefiting from what you have to offer. There are five foundation characteristics of a persuasive presentation.

1. Be interactive.
2. Be convincing.
3. Create a harm (a need).
4. Provide a choice.
5. Be competitive.

Be Interactive

Interaction simply means there must be a give-and-take between the presenter and the listener. To be persuasive, there cannot simply be one-way communication. The interactive or *transactional* aspect of a persuasive talk is what scholars call the *Socratic approach*. The speaker or salesperson must ask the right questions, listen to the answers, and respond before your conclusion.

If you want to persuade people, show the immediate relevance and value of what you're saying in terms of meeting

their needs and desires . . . successful collaborative negotiation lies in finding out what the other side really wants and showing them a way to get it, while you get what you want.
—Herb Cohen

One thing I practice with my workshop attendees is to have them try creating a presentation that answers common objections before a prospect can raise them. I call this approach *creating a proactive presentation*. It is preferable to a *reactive* presentation, which only informs the listeners and then invites their objections that must be overcome before the close.

Be Convincing

To be convincing, the presentation has to be logical. You will find it very difficult to create a compelling presentation without developing your argument. The following is a five-step process used to arrive at a logical persuasive argument:

1. Generate awareness.
2. State the problem.
3. Provide a solution.
4. Let them visualize change.
5. Call them to action.

Generating Awareness
When I refer to generating awareness, I mean making the prospect aware of his or her needs. People approach a salesperson with different levels of awareness about what they need or want. Sometimes too, customers have no understanding at all of the product or service. Depending on how much they know, we have to help them out. How many times have you ever worked with people who didn't know what they needed or how you could help?

Stating the Problem
The reason most people buy products is because they have a need or problem. The product or service solves or relieves

them of their problem. Generally, the problem is defined in terms of time, money, or an emotional need.

Providing a Solution

The salesperson needs to show prospective clients how the product or service being sold provides a solution to their problems. Providing the solution is a necessary element of creating a convincing, logical argument. If you are going to make your clients aware of their problems, you owe it to them to relieve their stress. You do this by providing a solution—buying your product or service. Doing so should save them time, money, or perhaps their sanity.

Have you ever heard the objection that your product/service costs too much? The following story offers at least one response that is effective in overcoming this type of objection.

How Much Is Your Time, Money, or Sanity Worth?

I travel a lot and am usually in a rush when checking out of a hotel. It's not uncommon for me to leave something behind, and this time it was my running shoes—one running shoe, to be exact. When I arrived home, I told my mother I needed to buy another pair, and she suggested we go to the local warehouse discount store where she holds a membership, versus our local mall, because I would save so much money.

I had never shopped at one of these warehouse clubs before and wasn't expecting to have to park a half-mile away. Nevertheless, I made the hike to the entrance, where I was stopped by an employee who asked to see my membership card. So my mom began fishing through her purse for the card. People began piling up behind us, then pushed around us to get inside. Finally Mom produced the card, and we were allowed to enter.

Since there is no shoe department, we wandered around looking for someone to ask where they keep the running shoes. Well, there were no clerks either; at least I couldn't find one. Finally I saw a big stack of shoes. Since they weren't in any order, I had to paw through the entire pallet to find my size. Great! Size $6^1/_2$—I was in luck. I opened the box, but inside there was only one shoe. So I dug around some more and found another box in my size. I tucked it under my arm and headed toward the checkout counter. The line must have had 15 people in it, and they all had huge carts full of merchandise. I waited in line for more than 20 minutes just to buy one pair of shoes. Then, when we got up to the cashier, he wouldn't take my credit card. It turned out the store didn't accept most major cards. We finally made it back to the car and realized we had wasted nearly an hour to save less than $10. Besides that, I was exhausted and in a terrible mood.

About a month later, I came home from another trip and, guess what? My car had been broken into and my new shoes stolen. The thought of going back to the warehouse store almost made me ill. I thought to myself, "This time, I'm going to South Coast Plaza" (one of the leading Southern California shopping malls). I got in my car, drove over to the store, and pulled up in front of a valet waiting outside. He opened the door, asked me how long I would be, and, smiling, took my car keys before presenting me with a receipt. I proceeded right into the store with no hassle about parking, no long trek from the lot—I just stepped right into the store. I walked directly to the shoe department where a clerk politely asked me what I was interested in wearing. I told him the brand and the size, and in less than a minute, I had a shoe on my foot. "Perfect," I said, and he asked me whether I would like to pay by cash or credit card. He took my credit card (I didn't even have to get out of my seat) and asked me if I wanted to take the shoes with me, or if I would like to have them shipped. Delighted, I asked him to ship them. He returned with my card, the charge and shipping slips for me to sign, and I was out of there!

I tipped the valet a dollar, slipped behind the wheel, and I was back on the road. I had saved maybe 40 minutes (that I could use putting together my next presentation) and I was in a great frame of mind. Was it worth the extra $10? You bet! So any time someone says your product or service costs too much, simply show them how it saves them time or helps preserve their sanity, which in the long run can also save them money. What is their time worth? The extra 40 minutes was worth a lot more to me than the $10. Did the warehouse club save me money or did it actually cost me money?

Visualizing Change

As a sales professional, you must help prospects visualize change. You have to take them from their present condition to that enhanced lifestyle you envision for them. Unless they can see themselves moving into a new dimension, they won't be convinced your product or service is necessary.

Call to Action

The final logical element in preparing a persuasive presentation is the call to action. This is the most important of the five steps. If you don't tell customers what you want them to do, they may misinterpret your message. They might not buy anything at all. They could even buy from someone else. You can't afford to take that chance. If you have developed the earlier part of your presentation in a convincing way, the customer already agrees with you and therefore the call to action sounds completely appropriate.

Create a Harm

The nature of a persuasive presentation means it tries to change people from believing in one set of ideas to having faith in another. It challenges the status quo by promoting a set of values not yet shared by the listener. It refutes existing ideas that may be held by the customers or audience. The persuasive presentation allows you to compete successfully for your client's allegiance. Clients may realize they could use a product or service similar to yours but may not have sufficient motivation to buy it. If they do decide to buy, will they shop for other products only to return to yours because it is best?

In the past, the answer was to sell consumers on features and benefits. Selling with features and benefits alone is more difficult today. In competitive markets, people often tend to eliminate the extras because they think they can't afford them or that they are unnecessary. They will purchase what they feel they need. The salesperson must develop a sense of urgency in the mind of the client in order to stimulate action. Unfortunately, there is no sense of urgency in a features-and-benefits presentation. For a prospect to understand why he or she must acquire our product or service, we must create a need or point out the *harm* likely to occur if they don't use what we have to offer. In the new century, a salesperson's job is to *create* needs, not just to do a needs analysis.

In order to act, clients must be convinced they can't get along without the product, service, or person. To convince them, the salesperson today can create a harm. What is a harm? I learned the term from a debate coach who taught me how to build an effective case, and I have been unable to find another word that better describes this technique. It is a tool used by debaters, attorneys, and politicians that sales and business professionals can employ to build arguments and make a case before a prospect or audience. A harm is the problem your customer or listener might encounter if they don't buy your product, service, or point of view. *A harm is the terrible, horrible thing that is going to happen to your client or prospect if they don't work with you, if they don't work with your company, and if they don't do it now.* A harm is merely a trigger to a thought process that will help build your persuasive case.

To create a harm that will help sell your product or service in today's challenging marketplace, ask yourself what would happen to your clients if they didn't work with you and your company? What would happen if they didn't do it now?

Defending Mr. Smith

Anyone can create a harm, no matter what the situation. The example I like to use in my seminars comes from the courtroom where our defendant, Mr. Smith, is on trial for murder. If you were the prosecutor, you would argue to the jury that it must convict Smith or he will be free to commit another horrible crime. The harm is that the population will be at risk if the jury releases Smith back on the streets.

If you were Smith's defense attorney, however, you would tell jurors that any murderer should be put behind bars. However, since Smith didn't do it, the jury will be convicting an innocent man. The real killer, meanwhile, will remain at large, free to murder again. The harm is that the jury will have committed a gross miscarriage of justice by imprisoning an innocent man, not to mention failing in its responsibility of fairly trying one of its peers.

No matter which side of the case you represent, you can create a harm to support your position. The same rules apply to a persuasive sales presentation. The whole point of creating harms is to build a sense of need in the mind of the client.

While it may seem harsh, every day we face the prospect of dealing with harms. Unfavorable situations are depicted through advertising on radio and television, in newspapers and magazines. The creation of harms in the media is a very clear adaptation to changes in economic conditions from the 1980s and 1990s to 2000 and beyond. The purpose is to create consumer needs.

I don't mean to suggest that there aren't significant elements of features-and-benefits selling, consultative selling, and value-added selling. The problem with all these approaches, however, is that in the course of executing them people sometimes stop being persuasive—in essence they stop selling. Overreliance on these techniques often gives the sales professional an excuse to be too informative.

The features-and-benefits approach to selling was popular back in the 1980s when people had plenty of money to throw around and did so without reservation. The more features and benefits something had, the more somebody wanted it. And that's why we learned to sell that way. People piled on the value-added services because they wanted to strengthen the significance of their product. As people decided they would purchase only what they felt they needed, the landscape changed. As we move beyond 2000 I think you will find that this is extremely evident, not only in the commercials, but also in the way we buy our products and services. Everything is tied to need.

Using a Harm to Sell Mouthwash

In the 1980s, a widely known mouthwash company promoted the features and benefits of their product. People were shown kissing in a variety of situations, and the message was: If you use this mouthwash, someone will want to—and most likely will—kiss you.

You would see several couples kissing in a variety of situations because kissing helps to illustrate the features-and-benefits factor of using the mouthwash. What's the feature? The breath-freshening action. What's the benefit? Everybody will want to kiss you. That's how most of the campaigns went. They were based on features-and-benefits selling. As we move into 2000 and beyond, the mouthwash commercial becomes quite different. Why? Because the mouthwash companies needed to create a greater need for buying mouthwash. Now you see Mr. and Mrs. Jones lying in bed. The alarm clock goes off, they wake up, they roll over in bed to say good morning, and this hideous gray fog comes out of their mouths. They immediately put their hands over their faces and say, "Good morning." Then they scamper off to separate bathrooms where they use their mouthwash. A minute later, they come back together again and then kiss. They didn't get rid of the feature and benefit, but they created the need up front. They identified a harm—morning breath!

Now pretend for a minute that you are pushing your shopping cart through the grocery store while thinking, "No, I don't want to add to my grocery bill by buying mouthwash." All of a sudden, the image of the gray fog comes into your mind, and you think to yourself, "Do I really want the eyes of my spouse to swell up with tears when I roll over in the morning to kiss him or her?" The answer to this question is probably no. So what do you do? You grab a bottle of mouthwash and toss it into your shopping cart. The reason you can justify the purchase now is because it's a need rather than just a desire. You avoid the harm by buying and using the product so you will have fresh breath. Buying the mouthwash is no longer a luxury. The viewer needs it in case he or she has morning breath, which most of us do. The advertisement still promotes the feature and benefit of kissing, but does so at the end.

Creating a Need for Cellular Phones

One of the all-time classic illustrations of creating a harm to sell more of a product comes from the cellular phone industry. Remember when cellular phones first came out? They were considered an expensive luxury item. When you saw the advertising campaigns, you would see an important-looking businessman with his chauffeur-driven car traveling down a busy street. He would call in for messages, he would call his wife, and he would call for dinner. The cellular phone, then known as a car phone, was promoted as a luxury. But the phone companies were not penetrating the market. The phones were sold as an upscale item to the wealthy, and some people even thought of them as pretentious. So the phone companies needed to change their image in order to sell to a larger market. (I can almost imagine a group of advertising agency creative types sitting around a conference table saying, "Okay, what terrible, horrible thing is going to happen if our customers don't carry cellular phones?")

Subsequently, the commercials began depicting a businesswoman driving her car along a major metropolitan city street. Steam is coming up through a street grate from the subway below. It appears to be about 10 or 11 o'clock at night. There aren't many people out on the streets. As she drives along, she turns a corner and, suddenly, her car breaks down. Now, she is sitting in her car and she looks off in the distance where she sees a pay phone. She is about to get out of the car when she looks again and realizes there are several hoodlums lurking around the phone booth. One has on a gangland-style bandana, another one has a big chain hanging from his belt to his wallet, and another is swaggering around with a bottle in a paper bag. She gets a fearful look on her face, and we viewers think as we watch the commercial, "Don't get out of the car!"

The commercial then stops and the same beginning scene replays. It's the same woman driving the same car down the same street. She turns that same corner; again her car breaks down. She looks around; she sees the pay phone. She looks again; she sees the hoodlums. But this time she glances down and looks at her cellular phone. She picks it up, dials for roadside service, and never has to get out of her car. The ad makes a cellular phone a necessity—a life-saving tool to be used in case of emergency.

They created a need with this campaign by identifying a harm. Now, do you think the campaign was aimed only at women? No, men responded well to it too. That is because men can't be with their sisters, girlfriends, and wives 24 hours a day. In case of an emergency, you have to have a cell phone to be safe—your life could depend upon it. Now the price becomes irrelevant.

Sales professionals sometimes worry that prices for their products or services are too high. But it is not that the price is too high; it is that the persuasive arguments have not been strong enough. How do you build your persuasive case? Identify the harm to establish a need. I'm not saying get rid of features and benefits. Establish what your three most persuasive arguments are up front for why the customer should work with you and your company, and why they should do it now. Then add your features and benefits, and then incorporate your value-added-services. If you build your presentations like this, you will overcome the biggest mistake that most professionals make when presenting, and that is that they have become far too informative rather than persuasive.

Tire commercials offer another good example of how advertisers create harms and therefore the need to buy their products. The awful thing that could happen to you if you don't own a particular brand of tire is strongly suggested by an abrupt stop just before a major accident is about to occur.

Automobile makers create a harm in the minds of TV viewers when they show a mannequin being tossed around inside a crashing car. The harm is that if you are not in one of their cars and you get in an accident like the one depicted, you could be crushed.

How to Identify a Harm

If I were sitting down with my debate coach back in college, and we were trying to create persuasive arguments to build a case, the first thing we would do is say, "Alright, what is the harm? What is the need?" We would identify the harm in order to identify the need so that we could create a persuasive case. And you can easily see this in the mouthwash example. First of all, they have to identify the harm, in order to create the need. So, what's the terrible, horrible thing that will happen if you don't use this mouthwash? You could have bad breath and nobody would want to kiss you. So, they have identified the harm. Now they have the need—to avoid morning breath and avoid offending anybody. (To create a need, ask yourself what terrible, horrible thing would happen if your client didn't work with you, work with your company, and they didn't do it now?)

To better understand how to create harms, look for them in TV commercials; they permeate the media. Even milk commercials have shifted in this direction. Back in the 1980s, "Milk, it does a body good" was a big features-and-benefits campaign to sell milk. Although it was a very effective campaign, since many of us remember the commercial, consider the later campaign: A man is lying in a hospital bed in a full body cast. He's absolutely incapacitated, but somebody gives him a chocolate chip cookie. He begins suffering because he doesn't have any milk to wash it down and he can't speak to ask for any. The commercial creates an image in your head that you will suffer if you don't have enough milk. It creates a little harm by making you imagine what it would be like to eat a dry chocolate chip cookie, desire milk to wash it down, yet not be able to have any.

One series of milk commercials features the cast of TV's sitcom *Frasier* talking about how Americans are losing calcium because they don't consume enough calcium or vitamins in their diets. Then they talk about how you need to drink milk because of its benefits. They created the need up front and added features and benefits at the end.

68

Use a Harm to Provide a Choice

By creating a harm we create a choice for the customer. Sometimes we have to be very specific in defining our client's options. The most frequently cited harm is the risk of working with someone other than ourselves—someone who easily could be less than satisfactory. Everyone has had poor service from a vendor. If customers don't work with you, they run the risk of working with someone less *efficient, effective, ethical, timely, friendly,* and *enthusiastic.*

Be Competitive but Don't Overdo It

One risk in creating choices for the prospect, particularly with a harm, is in overdoing it. We never want to denounce a competitor; neither do we want to create an undue sense of duress in the prospect while creating our harm. Granted, there is a fine line between the two. With practice, presenting a harm that provides the customer with a choice becomes second nature.

Of course you would never use the term *harm* in a presentation itself. It is just a word to trigger the mindset of someone building a persuasive argument.

Some people may want to use only one or two harms, while others will find the opportunity to build their entire presentation around a series of harms. Remember, this is just one of many instruments you can use to make your presentation persuasive. In the following chapters, we will discuss additional tools you can employ in your efforts to persuade your clients to take action.

Overview

- Mistake Number 2, the most common mistake that most professionals make when presenting, is that their presentations have become far too informative rather than persuasive.

- There are three presentation types or categories—informative, persuasive, and ceremonial. If you are on a job interview, it's a persuasive talk; you want them to hire you! All sales presentations are persuasive.
- There are five foundation characteristics of a persuasive presentation:
  1. It must be interactive.
  2. It must be convincing.
  3. It should incorporate *harms* to develop a need to build the persuasive argument.
  4. It must provide choice without duress.
  5. It must be competitive.
- There is a five-step process to logically persuade a listener:
  1. Generate awareness.
  2. State the problem.
  3. Provide a solution.
  4. Allow the listener to visualize the change.
  5. Employ a call to action.
- Don't overdo it—always remember to build a factual, credible, logical case delivered with integrity and class.

Next: Having reviewed the biggest mistake sales professionals make—providing too much information and not being persuasive—we turn to the problem of misusing your allotted time. In the next chapter we will look at the mechanics of exactly how to put together a powerful, persuasive presentation.

Mistake Number 3:
Misusing the Allotted Time

*Dost thou love life? Then do not squander time; for that's
the stuff life is made of . . .*

—Benjamin Franklin

Why Is This a Big Mistake?

Now that we recognize the importance of planning what we
are going to say and have selected an appropriate format
for our delivery, we still have to construct our presentation.
It is at this point that we need to be concerned about how
much time we spend on our listeners.

It is the time factor that really throws a lot of people off
their game, and speakers can go either way—too short or
too long. I recently watched as the head of a large publishing firm gave his sales staff the rundown on the company's
fall titles. He was supposed to speak briefly on each book in
order to get the sales team fired up for promoting the new

catalog to bookstore buyers, owners, and managers. He was scheduled to speak for an hour, but ended up talking about each title for a mere 30 seconds. Everyone expressed delight the meeting was over so soon. But all was not well with his presentation. With such brief descriptions, how much ammunition did the sales force really have before going out into the field to sell the company's products?

Yet when an individual talks too long, he or she is often perceived as long-winded, and the audience loses interest. The speaker may fail to get to the point, and the presentation certainly does not come across as quick, snappy, sharp, or dazzling.

> *Who is it that can make muddy water clear? But if allowed to remain still, it will gradually become clear of itself . . . be sparing of speech, and things will come right of themselves.*
> —Lao-Tzu

To be an effective speaker, you have to exercise control over how much time your presentation really requires. To be good at this, you are going to have to practice your timing. You should have a sense for what a five-minute talk is like and how it differs from one that is 10 minutes.

Determine how much time you have. Then develop a presentation that fits within those parameters. If you have a 30-minute presentation and you know that there are six components to a presentation, you might divide the six into 30, and you know that each component should be allotted about five minutes. In order to do this, I suggest that you practice giving your presentation in advance. Don't just stand up there and wing it. Second, you should be able to cover every important argument with an illustration and know what to include and what to delete in case you are asked at the last minute to shorten or lengthen your presentation.

Organizing

Learning how to organize a talk is key to controlling its length. It also is central to creating a persuasive case. Constructing it is easy when you understand the formula. Delivering it with the skill of an eighteenth-century orator will take a little more time, but with practice you will be able to accomplish that too.

Skilled organization of your argument, deft use of speech supports and transitions, and a clear call to action will make your message irresistible to your audience. You can outline your presentation, write it out word for word, or do both. However, you should use a pencil and paper (or word processor) as you develop your ideas. Let's take a look at just how you will build your first truly dazzling presentation.

The easiest way for us to break it down is to consider the components of an average presentation. The outline of your presentation includes:

- Introduction.
- Body with main three points:
  1. Why choose you?
  2. Why your company?
  3. Why now?
- Conclusion.
- Close.

The body of your presentation should have three main points. Then there are ultimately six components to your presentation. The introduction has two functions: grabbing the audience's attention and telling them where you're going. The main points of your presentation contained within the body should tell why the listener should work with you, why your company, and why now. The conclusion of your presentation is a wrap-up. It's where you go back and tell them what you told them. This is followed by the close, your specific call to action—what you want them to do as a result of your message.

Writing the Introduction

The introduction is one of the most important parts of your presentation and consists of four elements. Assigning the right amount of time to the introduction will rivet your audience on what you say next. Know what you are going to say in that first 35 seconds that will make your audience sit up and go, "Wow! This might be really different," or "Gee! This talk might be unique compared to all the rest of them." There's nothing better than your being a pleasant surprise. The introduction also informs your listeners where you are going. This is where you set up a mental menu of what you are going to cover in your presentation.

Grabbing Attention

First is a bold statement to attract attention. This is a statement everyone can understand. It should have a universal context. Frequently, it is followed by an *anchor*—a way to unify the audience and provide a point of common reference. The larger and more diverse the group, the more challenging it becomes to find an effective anchor. Nevertheless, most groups have something in common. When giving a one-on-one presentation, you should be able to determine what you have in common with your client or prospect. This is best done with a short, preferably humorous, personal story or quotation.

Including the Credibility Enhancer

Next you should include a sentence or two to enhance your credibility. This can be a statistic, a published fact from an authoritative journal, or a quotation by an authority or famous person.

Making It Important

Follow up with a statement to promote the importance of what you are about to say. Why does your client need to react now? What evidence, scientific or otherwise, can you provide that will convince this person that you are about to say something important?

Including a Background Statement

Fourth comes a background statement. This gives your listeners further reason to pay attention to what you have to say. It sets the context for your claims from a historical perspective and helps establish you as an authority.

Signposting

One of the techniques for successful delivery is called *signposting*. This means using phrases to let the audience know where you are going with your presentation. It is a way to provide a mental road map to listeners so they can better understand what you say. A signpost gives advance notice of the direction you are taking so that when you get there, your audience will understand you and be ready for the next point. Think of it as a direct summary statement delivered in advance of the supporting facts.

Transition

The background statement and signposting are followed by a smooth transition designed to take the listener into the body, or main part, of the presentation. A transition is a sentence that triggers in the minds of your listeners the fact that you are moving to another subject.

Writing the Body

A listener typically will remember only three main points as a result of any presentation, and you want them to be the ones you choose, not three random facts that they happen to catch in passing. So what are those three things? For the sales professional, the body needs to answer three questions:

1. Why should clients work with you?
2. Why should they work with your company?
3. Why should they do it now?

Each of these body points should have five sections:

1. Your argument stating what you want to say or prove.
2. Your sources of justification.
3. The reasons why your argument will work.
4. What risk the prospect will face if he or she doesn't work with you (a harm).
5. The features and benefits of your product or service.

The final section is followed by a transition to the second body point—why the prospect should work with your company. A transition separates this segment from the third and final point—why he or she should do it now.

Conclusion

You may have guessed that once you have finished supporting all three of your body points you want to end with a conclusion. The conclusion is a wrap-up. This is where you go back and tell them what you told them so your listeners will retain a greater amount of information. Then you close with a specific call to action. The conclusion, however, is not quite as simple as we remember it from school. It has up to five distinct sections:

1. Summary of the information already presented.
2. Appeal for your listener to take action.
3. Statement of your personal intent (what specific steps you will take to move the transaction forward).
4. Reference back to your introduction (to close with strength).
5. Powerful new story to emphasize your point (optional).

Close

In addition to the wrap-up or conclusion, every presentation must have a close. The close is your specific call to action—what you want your listener to do as a result of your message or what your client has to do in order to complete the transaction. For example, this could be signing the contract or setting the next appointment time. One of the nine biggest sales presentation mistakes for many people is that they conclude, but they don't close. We will look at this distinction in greater detail in Chapter 6.

Presentation Guide

The Easy-to-Use Presentation Guide given on pages 78 and 79 is a summary outline showing how to create a persuasive presentation. After reviewing it, try practicing developing a talk that you can deliver during your next sales presentation. Use the blank Easy-to-Use Presentation Outline Form beginning on pages 91 and 92 to help organize your ideas.

Making this type of outline in advance of your presentation is essential. Benefits are so great that I constantly stress them to students who go through our training programs. They include:

- Providing clarity and control of the information.
- Preventing the speaker from straying off course.
- Allowing a chance for you to share your knowledge, thus establishing your credibility.
- Promoting audience interaction and encouraging them to think of questions and objections (also helps the audience to formulate positive images and set personal objectives).
- Helping the client (or audience) retain more information due to the clear, logical format.
- Helping to build a logical case for why the client should work with you and your company, and why they should do so now.

Easy-to-Use Presentation Guide

1. Introduction

Statements to:

1. Grab the audience's attention.
2. Focus that attention (short, preferably humorous, personal story or quotation).
3. Enhance your credibility of purpose (your goals for the relationship).
4. Make what you say important (why your client should listen to you).
5. Provide a background statement.
6. Signpost (to tell them where you are going and what your three points will be).

Transition—lets them know you are moving into the body of your presentation.

Body (typically has three points):

In the body you will build the overall argument of why a business transaction needs to be completed. You list separate "points." Each one has its own arguments.

1. Why your prospects should work with you.
2. Why they should work with your company.
3. Why they should act now.

2. Body Point 1

Explain why your prospects should work with you (as an individual). Think of the three most important reasons.

1. Your arguments (what you want to prove or say).
2. Sources of justification.
3. Good reasons why your argument works.
4. The harm (what risk they will assume if they don't work with you).
5. Your own list of features and benefits.

Transition—lets them know you are moving into the next point.

3. Body Point 2

Give a rundown of why they should work with your company.

1. Your arguments (what you want to prove or say).
2. Sources of justification.

3. Good reasons why your argument works.
4. The harm (what risk they will take if they don't work with your company).
5. Your company's features and benefits.

Transition—lets them know you are moving into the next point.

4. Body Point 3

Tell your clients why they should act now.

1. Your arguments (what you want to prove or say).
2. Sources of justification.
3. Good reasons why your argument works.
4. The harm (what risk they will take if they don't do it now).
5. Features and benefits of immediate action.

Transition—lets them know you are beginning to wrap up your presentation.

5. Conclusion

1. Summary of information.
2. Appeal to take action.
3. Statement of personal intent (what specific steps you will take to move the transaction forward).
4. Reference back to the introduction (to close with power).
5. New story to emphasize your point (optional).

At this point, you may want to answer questions.

6. Close

Now comes your specific call to action. What is it you want your audience to do as a result of your presentation? Typical examples of options you might offer your client at the close of your presentation include:

1. Signing the contract.
2. Setting the next appointment time.

If the client won't make the commitment right now and sign on the dotted line, it is important to produce your calendar and set a future appointment date. Don't let the client put you off until later if you can possibly avoid it.

- Helping map the course of your presentation so you know where to put stories and illustrations (these contribute to making clear and memorable points, resulting in a more persuasive and polished presentation. We will discuss these more in Chapter 5).
- Ensuring your overall presentation will be professional.

How Do We Control Time?

Now, everything would be wonderful if you always had adequate time, but sometimes you are pushed into a corner where someone tells you, "I know you are supposed to have a half hour, but actually you only have 20 minutes."

What do you do now?

You go directly back to your mental outline. One of the things that I recommend is that you use an extemporaneous format, which means that you speak from an outline. Then you can ask yourself, "What are the key points that I really need to focus on in my presentation now that my time has been shortened?" You look at your outline and pick out the key points. You decide what the less important details are. Maybe you can drop a statistic or a testimonial. Still make the points that you must, in a beautiful and illustrative fashion, but condense them so that the presentation meets the time constraints your client or management has imposed.

Sample Persuasive Presentation Outlines

On pages 82 to 88, you will find two sample presentation outlines for your review. The first is a *long presentation outline* which offers a detailed look at a comprehensive presentation. The second is a simplified *short presentation outline* that will help you lay out the basics or core skeleton of a presentation. Both versions of the outline are effective depending on your comfort level with the material and the amount of practice you commit to the presentation prior to its delivery. If you follow the steps in the outlines, you will have created a very persuasive and powerful presentation that will make it much easier to close, and your listeners will be much more inclined to heed your call to action.

Note: Every argument does not need to have a harm. And every body point does not need to have three subpoints. Use your own judgment and personal interpretation. Try new approaches, and use your creativity. Consider the following hypothetical opportunity for preparing a presentation.

Scenario

Imagine a board of trustees is bringing in four investment management organizations to evaluate and select a new investment advisor. Each management organization will be given 30 minutes to present a general overview of its company. Your company has been selected as one of the four firms under consideration. Your competitors are not disclosed. You find out you have been selected to deliver the presentation on behalf of your company only 24 hours prior to the meeting. The outcome of this meeting will determine the two finalists who will be invited back to deliver a second, more specific presentation.

AUDIENCE ANALYSIS

Audience: The members of the board of trustees, typically a conservative group.

Audience size: 8 to 12.

Average age range: 30 to 65 years old.

Male/female ratio: 60 percent male and 40 percent female.

Attitude of audience: Marginally satisfied with current investment advisor.

How informed is audience: Experts in their vocation but novices in the investment field.

LOGISTICAL INFORMATION

Facility: Meeting room at a college campus.

Visual aids: Overhead projector and screen are available. You may also use handouts and flip charts or white board. All other materials you will need to provide.

Mistake Number 3: Misusing the Allotted Time

(If you want more sophisticated audiovisual equipment, you must provide it.)

Time: 30-minute presentation with an additional 15 minutes afterward for Q&A.

Your speaking position: Determined at the meeting.

Speaker: Ryan Kelly, Spectrum Asset Management Inc., Newport Beach, California.

LONG PRESENTATION OUTLINE

I. **Introduction**
   A. In Holland in 1636 one rare tulip cost 4 bushels of wheat, 8 pigs, 12 sheep, 5 kegs of beer, a thousand pounds of cheese, a bed, a fine suit, and a silver cup.
   B. Imagine the following story: That same year, the captain of a ship carrying foreign cargo sees an interesting looking onion that he thinks looks out of place among the fine silks they are transporting. The captain eats the onion with his lunch. When the ship arrives on shore, the captain is thrown in jail for almost a year for eating a tulip that would have fed and paid for the captain's ship and crew for a year. If the captain had known the value of the tulip, he surely would not have eaten it. The following year that same tulip had lost 95 percent of its value and would trade for only the cost of one sheep.

II. **Main Point of Presentation**
   A. To understand your responsibility as a board member is to be the captain of a ship—your ship—and your greatest concern is to protect and increase your investment portfolio. At Spectrum we know which tulips not to eat, how many sheep it should cost to buy a tulip, and when to sell your tulips for the greatest return on your investment. We want to represent you and your financial interests. Our goal is to earn your business and construct a strategy designed for your specific needs based on our research and experience and your comfort level.

III. **My Statement Which Makes What I Say Important**
   A. We truly have a unique advantage to meet your specific needs. *Explanation*: There are thousands of investment

82

management organizations and opportunities. You need to select just one. So why Spectrum Asset Management?

1. We educate you. We help you understand what you don't know (short film, three minutes).
2. We are a David in a world of Goliaths working for you. Surely most of us have heard the biblical tale from the book of Samuel about David versus Goliath.

   a. *Illustration*: Two opposing forces, the Philistines and Israelites, were facing each other poised for battle. Goliath, a Philistine warrior, was a giant of tremendous strength and size. He challenged the Israelites to a one-on-one fight against their best warrior, winner-take-all. But Goliath inspired such fear among the Israelites that none of their warriors would step forward to fight him because they were certain to die and lose their cause. After a number of days, a young Israelite shepherd stepped forward and said he would fight Goliath as a testament to his faith in God. As the two faced each other on the battlefield, Goliath scoffed at the young man standing before him with neither sword nor shield. And as we all know, David took out his sling, loaded it with a rock, swung the stone around above his head and let fly. He knocked Goliath to the ground, then slew him. In the investment business, there are a lot of Goliaths. We are David working for you in a world of Goliaths.

IV. **Signpost**

A. My goal is to provide a brief presentation on how our company, Spectrum Asset Management, can meet your investment management organization needs. Initially I would like to tell you a little bit about myself. Second, I would like to share with you the unique benefits of working with our company. Finally, I would like to discuss the advantages of working with Spectrum now.

V. **Why Ryan?**

A. As a principal in the firm, I have a vested interest in your success. If you don't do well, I don't do well. However, what does the standard broker get when he or she gives bad advice? A commission (harm—expand on this). If you do well, I do well because I'm an owner (explanation and discussion of features and benefits of working with a principal of the firm versus a standard investment manager).

B. I don't use trade talk; I use simple terms that are clear, concise, direct, and crafted in plain English so you can understand everything that is going on with your portfolio (no industry jargon). In addition, in our business there are two types of people: Those who tell you what you want to hear and those who tell you what you should hear (harm—explanation of why when you work with Ryan, you get the straight talk you need to make effective decisions).

C. When I say I provide more than just our core service, I really do, at no extra charge. I am a resource to you (argument/point). I can provide advice on the quality of a portfolio, on transferring stock certificates, on determining the value of an arcane stock, and on estate planning, and help in leveraged buyouts, and in setting up charitable trusts (explain with features and benefits).

VI. **Why Spectrum?**

A. We are unique because we specialize in individual portfolio management accounts, in the half-million to $20-million-dollar range (argument/point).

B. What does that mean to you? Because of our specialization, we can outperform our competitors in customization, service, and price as well as defensive strategies. For example, imagine that the goal of your investment advisor is to bake you a cookie. The large bakeries in this industry roll out the dough and then take out a cookie cutter and cut the same-shaped cookie for everyone. What we specialty bakeries do is make custom cookies. If you need a gingerbread man, that's what we cut. If you need a cake, then that's what we bake. If you need something that says, "Happy Birthday, Son," that's what you get. The large firms will serve you plain-vanilla wafers when you need a gingerbread man (harm). At Spectrum, we provide our clients custom-baked cookies at a better price than our competitors' mass-produced cookies. *Evidence*: We currently provide this customized service for a number of clients. If you would like to speak with any of them, we would be happy to arrange it.

C. We are strong defensive players (argument/point). If you have $1 million and it's worth $700,000 the next week, you don't care what your relative performance is. You care that your money is gone. Our goal is to avoid risk (additional point). So we hit base hits, not home runs. Babe Ruth in his day had the most home runs but also had the most strikeouts. In baseball that's fine, but in investments it takes too long to make up lost capital (harm). Hypothetically, if you lose 50 percent of your assets you have to earn 100 percent on the remainder to get even, whereas if you lose only 20 percent of your assets you have to earn 25 percent, which is much more achievable. Naturally, our focus is on a zero-capital-loss strategy.

VII. Why Now?

A. Why should you switch to working with Spectrum versus your current asset management company now? Everyone gets religion after the devil shows up—why not get it beforehand? Let's say you have a million dollars and six months from now it's worth $700,000. How would that make you feel? "Would have, could have, and should have" are the three richest men in the world. Sometimes doing nothing can cost you a lot more than taking action (harm), because the time to take action is before things hit the fan. Afterward it's too late.

B. We protect and defend your principal the second you become a client, through nonemotional exit strategies. In our industry, the biggest weakness that individuals and professional investors have is that they are bad sellers. They don't sell when they should. On all of our positions, we have a sell alert and a sell stop, which ensure that we avoid significant loss, and we take the emotion out of the selling decision. You get the security of protecting your principal with all the advantages of growth potential, which means less risk to you, the client.

C. We provide solid, conservative growth strategy. Unfortunately, the majority of our clients come to us after they have already suffered a great deal of pain and loss. The reason is because most investment decisions are made reactively versus proactively.

D. *Illustration*: In 1994, all of Spectrum Asset Management's institutional accounts made money. Contrast this with the County of Orange that lost $12.7 billion and went into bankruptcy. If the County of Orange had been a client under the same management strategy we calculated, it would have *made* money. We protect you even in the worst of situations. The year 1994 was the worst in the government bond market since 1927. However, the government bond mutual fund managed by Spectrum finished number three in the country, which means that even in the worst of situations, our clients maintained their principal. We protect our clients' hard-earned dollars. We'd like to do the same for you.

VIII. Conclusion

A. Summary of information given (quickly review key points of presentation).

B. Appeal to take action:
1. Ask for the next appointment time to present a more in-depth case (ask for their business).

C. Statement of personal intent:
1. (What will you do to carry forth the business relationship?) Share how you will personally roll up your shirt sleeves to create a customized action plan to meet their specific needs and provide a detailed explanation of how to implement their investment strategy.

D. Reference to introduction: At Spectrum we are willing to do what it takes to earn your business. We would be honored to represent your account.

IX. Close

A. *Ask*: What do we want them to do as a result of this presentation? *Answer*: Invite Spectrum and Ryan Kelly to attend the next level of presentation opportunities. *Then ask*: How much money are they willing to commit in an initial advance? Will they sign a contract or set up the next appointment time right now?

SHORT PRESENTATION OUTLINE

I. **Introduction**
   A. Grab attention: Tulip analogy.
   B. Focus attention with short story: Captain eating-the-onion tale.
   C. Goals for the relationship: Earn their business and advise clients through knowledge, research, and experience.
   D. Why should they listen to you?
      1. We truly have a unique advantage to meet your specific needs. There are thousands of investment management organizations and opportunities. You need to select just one. So why Spectrum Asset Management?
         a. We educate you. We help you understand what you don't know.
         b. We are a David working for you in a world of Goliaths.
         c. Provide background: Expand with two illustrations, the issues listed above.
         d. *Signpost*: Tell them where you are going and what your three points will be.
            (1) Why should they work with Ryan Kelly?
            (2) Why should they work with Spectrum Asset Management?
            (3) Why should they do it now?

II. **Body**
   A. Point 1: Why Ryan?
      1. As a principal in this firm, I have a vested interest in your success. If you don't do well, I don't do well.
      2. I forgo the trade talk: I use simple communication that is clear, concise, direct, and in plain English so you understand everything that is going on with your portfolio.
      3. When I say we provide more than just our core service, we really do.
   B. Point 2: Why Spectrum Asset Management?
      1. Brief company overview: To provide a solid foundation and general familiarity with the organization.

    2. We outperform our competition in terms of:
       a. Customization.
       b. Service.
       c. Price.
       d. Defense strategies.
  C. Point 3: Why now? Why should you switch now to working with Spectrum Asset Management versus your current asset management company?
    1. We protect and defend your principal—the moment you become a client—through nonemotional exit strategies.
    2. We provide a solid growth strategy.
    3. We protect you even in the worst of situations.

III. Conclusion
  A. Quickly review the key points of the presentation.
  B. Appeal to take action: Ask for the opportunity of a second appointment.
  C. Statement of personal intent: The goal of the second meeting would be to roll up our shirtsleeves and create an action plan and implement an investment strategy.

IV. Close
  A. Ask how much money they are willing to commit for an initial advance. Have them sign a contract or set up the next appointment time.

A Balanced Presentation

One of my mentors, Floyd Wickman, who is a legendary speaker and trainer, recounted how his mentor, Zig Ziglar, told him, "If you want to make a story or a presentation better, tell it shorter." Unfortunately, there is a common misconception that, "I've just got to make it really short, and then I've got to get out." There has to be a balance. That's why we say, *don't misuse the allotted time*. Balance means fully developing your ideas. Develop your thoughts, and then utilize the amount of time that you have been allotted, being respectful of the audience's time and attention span. Adults want information fast, they want it intensely, and they want it concisely—then they want to be out the door.

Getting Started with an Outline Form

By employing the format used in the Presentation Outlines you can create your own presentation. If you use the blank Presentation Opportunity General Information Sheet and Easy-to-Use Presentation Outline Form on pages 90 and 91–92 for planning and practicing your next talk, it will be easy to put together a winning presentation. You may want to make copies of this presentation outline form or put it into your computer. That way it will be easier to develop a new outline to meet the needs of each individual client. The more often you create an outline, the easier it will become.

The Overnight Presentation

Now that you know how to put together both short and long presentation outlines, imagine yourself in the following situation.

A Golden Opportunity

You are at your desk, it is 3:30 P.M., and you have at least a half-day's work to do before you go home. Your regional manager walks in.

"Joan, I know this is rather short notice, but I need someone to fill in for me tomorrow morning at the vice-president's staff meeting. I just got called back to headquarters, and my flight leaves tomorrow at 8:30 A.M. Can you help me out?"

"Sure," you reply, eager to please your manager, but with little idea of what is involved.

"Okay," she says. "Here's the deal. We have to sell the finance committee on the importance of funding the Bellwether Project. All budget requests must be in by tomorrow. Anything not submitted won't be considered for funding next year. If that happens, the project won't get started for

---

PRESENTATION OPPORTUNITY GENERAL INFORMATION SHEET

I. What is the goal of your presentation? _____

_____

_____

_____

II. Audience analysis information:

  1. Who are the listeners? _____

_____

  2. Audience size? _____

  3. Average age of group? _____

  4. Male/female ratio? _____

  5. Attitude of audience? _____

_____

  6. How informed is the audience? _____

_____

III. Logistical information:

  1. Facility: _____

  2. Visual aid requirements: _____

_____

  3. Amount of time allotted for presentation: _____

  4. Who speaks before/after you? _____

_____

EASY-TO-USE PRESENTATION OUTLINE FORM

Introduction

    1. _____

    2. _____

    3. _____

    4. _____

    5. _____

    6. _____

Transition_____

Body (the three main points to be covered)

    1. _____

    2. _____

    3. _____

Body Point 1

    1. _____

    2. _____

    3. _____

    4. _____

    5. _____

Transition _____

Body Point 2

    1. _____

    2. _____

(Continued)

EASY-TO-USE PRESENTATION OUTLINE FORM *(Continued)*

Body Point 2

    3. _____

    4. _____

    5. _____

Transition _____

Body Point 3

    1. _____

    2. _____

    3. _____

    4. _____

    5. _____

Transition _____

Conclusion

    1. _____

    2. _____

    3. _____

    4. _____

    5. _____

Close

    1. _____

    2. _____

three-and-a-half years. As it is now, it will be more than 18 months before we can get underway. We couldn't compile the material earlier because the contractor estimates weren't in yet."

"Well, what do I have to do?" you ask, slightly bewildered and a little alarmed that this is a critical presentation for which there is insufficient time to prepare.

"Just make sure the committee members understand the project, that they are convinced of its importance, and that all of them believe it will pay for itself over the next five years. It is absolutely vital, as you know. Here are all the materials." She drops eight huge file folders onto your desk. "Thanks, Joan. I won't forget this at your review."

As you watch her disappear around the corner, you think to yourself, *what do I do now?*

Career Boost

This could be your ticket to greener pastures. While it is not a typical sales scenario, we have included a section on the overnight presentation because it occurs frequently in business and may involve a sales presentation. Though you don't have time to produce a colorful videotape, and may not even have time to make view-graphs, you still can put together a convincing oral presentation that will knock the socks off the finance committee and achieve the objectives established by your manager. Considering the authority level of your audience, to say that a good performance before this committee might give your career a boost would be to understate the obvious. Before that can happen, however, you will have to impress them.

Getting the Job Done

The secret to a successful overnight presentation lies in carefully planning what to say. Use the blank Presentation Opportunity General Information Sheet and Easy-to-Use Presentation Outline Form beginning on page 90, review your facts and source materials, and you may find you can simply fill in the blanks. If you follow the outline, it will see you through to a successful conclusion. The result will be a logical, formulated, and convincing presentation.

Overview

- Mistake number 3 is *misusing the allotted time*. Effectively building a balanced presentation within specific time parameters is a key component in becoming a great presenter.
- Organization is the key to managing your presentation time more effectively.
- The typical presentation has six components: introduction, three body points, conclusion, and close.
- To balance your presentation's content with the time available to present it, you may want to divide the number of components in your presentation by the amount of time you have to deliver your message. For example, a 30-minute presentation divided by six components equals approximately five minutes per component.
- The overnight presentation is not impossible. Use the blank Presentation Opportunity General Information Sheet and extemporaneous Easy-to-Use Presentation Outline Form to help you get started. It could be a golden opportunity.

Next: Now that we know how a presentation should be constructed, and can therefore control how much time it takes to deliver, we can move on to the next common mistake that presenters make—providing inadequate support.

Mistake Number 4:
Providing Inadequate Support

If you would persuade, you must appeal to interest rather than intellect.

—Benjamin Franklin

M ost people when they give a presentation aren't able to completely win over their listeners because they don't provide adequate supporting material for their arguments. This undermines their credibility as well as their effectiveness at communicating the information. The simple truth is that opinion alone is not enough in most cases to allow your argument to persuade your listeners to act; you need to support what you say with a variety of facts and stories that appeal to your listeners' minds, hearts, and souls.

It is not uncommon for presentations to lack the kind of support it takes to build a strong case, but creatively illustrating your points will help bring your presentation to life.

As a result, your listeners will better understand and re-member what you are saying. In the new millennium, with the huge amount of information that will be available to the public, your clients will be better informed and more capa-ble of differentiating between your product or service and those of your competitors. To earn your clients' business, you will have to be highly credible and be able to build a case that meets the specific needs of the buyer or decision-maker. Incorporating speech supports into your presenta-tion will help you achieve that.

Speech supports include anecdotes, analogies, defini-tions, examples, stories, statistics, and testimonials. You should constantly be gathering these types of materials and keep them in a special *presentation ideas* file. As you incor-porate them into the skeleton or outline of your presenta-tion, your talk becomes much more fun to listen to.

Achieving Credibility

We like to think of ourselves as trustworthy and believable. However, the undeniable profit we receive from convincing someone to buy from us makes us suspect in the eyes of the client. Combine this with a profession whose history is re-plete with ethical breaches, and you begin to realize why it is terribly important to establish credibility. In the book, *Credibility: How Leaders Gain and Lose It, and Why People Demand It,* authors James M. Kouzes and Barry Z. Posner maintain: "Credibility is mostly about consistency between words and deeds. People listen to the words and look at the deeds. They measure the congruence. A judgment of credi-ble is handed down when the two are consonant."

Personal and Information Credibility

Your customer will evaluate both you and your information before deciding whether to believe you. Enhancing the credibility of both yourself and your material will help you be more persuasive. I can't overemphasize the importance of sounding believable. If your prospects do not believe in you or in what you are saying, they will have to be absolutely desperate before buying what you are selling.

If you do not positively believe in what you are selling or the service you represent, it will become apparent. Find something else that you can feel personally confident about representing. Your feelings must be aligned with your message.

Major Speech Supports

Not only will speech supports enhance your credibility, but they will also make your presentation sound a lot more interesting. Following is a list of the eight major speech supports:

1. Anecdote (story).
2. Analogy.
3. Definition.
4. Example.
5. Statistics.
6. Testimonial.
7. Hypothesis.
8. Rhetorical question.

When documented and used appropriately, speech supports can give your presentation the credibility otherwise achieved only by personally knowing your client. A speech replete with a variety of supports sounds solid. Documentation gives it credibility. Let's briefly discuss each of the supports so you understand what they are and how they work.

Anecdote

Among the most effective tools in your kit is the *anecdote*—a short, often humorous story, either real or fictitious. The anecdote allows you to take your message outside the business context with an illustration that anyone can understand. It entertains the listener and makes your point memorable. Using an anecdote also makes you, the speaker, seem warmhearted, down-to-earth, and likable.

Analogy

Analogy is the comparison of similar characteristics found in dissimilar circumstances. You might draw an analogy between an artery in a patient who has arteriosclerosis and a mountain stream gradually freezing in winter. Analogies are effective in explaining new material to your listeners because they provide them with reference points they already understand. Salespeople often explain new products and services to prospective customers. Analogies prove useful in bridging the gap between the old and the new.

Definition

Most of us already know that a *definition* is a statement of precise meaning or significance. Using definitions in a presentation can enhance the speaker's credibility. The client perceives the salesperson to be knowledgeable. Using a definition also reduces the chance for miscommunication.

Definitions may be important when you are using technical terms from a given industry. Or other terms you have to use could be colloquial and will need to be defined for your audience. Those who already know the definition will suddenly begin to feel a part of your world, thus enhancing your credibility. Definitions promote the customer's understanding of your meaning. They lead the customer toward seeing things the way you need them to be seen in order for you both to move forward.

Example

An *example* is one representative from a larger group. We often use examples to clarify general ideas. They may describe benefits or reduced risk. Frequently we use examples to show how something can be used. They might show how to avoid a problem that could take place in the future. You can use examples to describe situations that likely will happen if the client doesn't use your product or service (another way to reinforce a harm). You may want to illustrate the positive feelings or benefits the client will receive from your product. Specifics show how the product can increase pleasure, reduce pain, or save money or time. Remember that to be effective, your audience should be able to relate to the examples you cite in your presentation.

Statistics

We think of statistics as meaning numbers. More broadly, *statistics* is the system of mathematics associated with organizing and interpreting numerical data. Using statistics is a highly effective way of ensuring that what you say is credible. Yet the impact is dependent on how dramatic the numbers are. Too many statistics will put your audience to sleep. A good statistic, followed up by a good anecdote or testimonial, will make a strong impression.

Testimonial

When a statement testifying to a particular truth or fact is formally delivered or written down, we call it a *testimonial*. When we incorporate testimonials within our presentation, we have the weight of another person's reputation reinforcing what we are claiming.

A testimonial says, "Look, these people were nervous, just as you are; or these people had concerns, just as you do. They went ahead and did it anyway. Now look how happy they are. They even wrote me a letter of reference." The testimonial carries only as much weight with your prospect as the person who signed it. It is important therefore that a testimonial be appropriate.

Hypothesis

The *hypothesis* is an assumption we postulate to further our argument. We ask, "What if we could prove how this machine will pay for itself in six months? Would you buy it?" We create a hypothetical situation to explain our point.

Rhetorical Question

Frequently, a salesperson will want to ask the customer a *rhetorical question*—a question for which the answer is so obvious it needn't be stated. I might ask, "How many of you have heard your clients say, 'I want to think about it'?"

Such questions help create rapport with the audience. They provide a common bond by showing that you both are salt of the earth. Rhetorical questions say, "I'm a good person to listen to because I've been where you have been. I know the things you experience daily. I also can provide you with advice on other things to do in the future." This type of image gives you credibility.

Developing a Creative Sales Imagination

Creativity can solve almost any problem. The creative act, the defeat of habit, by originality, overcomes everything . . . "
—George Lois

Among the most frequently overlooked instruments in the sales professional's repertoire is a creative imagination. Whoever said sales doesn't demand originality? Conceiving effective, persuasive presentations for different audiences requires tremendous creative energy. While everyone has different levels of talent, people are creative by nature, and creativity can be enhanced like any other skill. It takes initiative and self-discipline. But a lot of times people say, "That sounds great, except, you know what Terri? I'm not that creative." Nonsense—of course you are; maybe you just haven't tapped into your creative right-brain functions lately when it comes to your business life.

Most of the time people get very linear when they think they are in *business mode*. They don't allow their personality and their creativity and energy back into the delivery of their message. Begin with creating an environment for yourself where your potential and your motivation are released.

Two Sources for Ideas

There are only two places from which ideas can come. You can either borrow them from someone else or originate them on your own. Most good ideas are a synthesis drawn from both sources. The renowned jurist, Oliver Wendell Holmes, wrote that an idea often is improved after being transplanted into the mind of another person. Improving upon someone else's idea is a creative and acceptable way to develop your own presentation style.

The important things are to be memorable and to be unique. Using your creative imagination to employ the speech supports discussed earlier means developing your own anecdotes and corroborating material to support your argument. The source for these often will be everyday life. Using your own personal stories allows your clients to know you better. Such stories are usually very interesting to listeners.

The following section presents my 12 keys for stimulating a more dynamic and creative presentation style. Each key will be illustrated in detail.

Happiness lies in the joy of achievement and the thrill of creative effort.

—Franklin D. Roosevelt

Twelve Keys to Developing a More Creative Sales Imagination

1. Establish a creative environment.
2. Read books.
3. Listen to tapes.
4. Read newspapers, journals, and magazines.
5. Create a brainstorming group.
6. Find a role model.

7. Attend courses, workshops, seminars, and conferences.
8. Watch TV and movies; go to comedy shows.
9. Evaluate other speakers.
10. Conduct customer and competitor interviews.
11. Join professional associations or committees.
12. Invite a mentor to lunch or dinner.

Creative Environment

Michael Jeffreys, a colleague, trainer, and noted public speaker, describes what happens when you are not in a creative environment by telling a story about crabs. If you were to catch several live crabs and place them in a bucket, you would never have to put a lid on the top for fear that the crabs were going to crawl out and escape. If one of them were to try to climb out, the other live crabs would reach up and grab it and pull it back in. Crabs apparently don't like other crabs getting ahead of them.

However, if you were to catch a single crab and put it in a bucket, you then would have to put a lid over it because the individual crab will crawl out, or die trying. Now the question we have to ask ourselves is: Are we sitting in a bucket of crabs? If we were left on our own, would we actually achieve more?

We all have heard the saying "misery loves company." Well, mediocrity loves company, too. The thought is, "Okay, let's all be mediocre together, then nobody can put any pressure on us to achieve more!" If you are the crab who does try to break out of the pot, then you have to deal with all the other crabs that will reach up and pull you back. Why? Because if you try to break out, it puts pressure on all the other crabs in the bucket. They have two choices. They can either rally and keep up with you, or they can reach up and grab you and pull you back down. It's a lot easier for all those mediocre crabs in the bottom of the pot to reach up and grab the individual who is trying to leave than it is for the one ambitious crab to pull everyone else upward and onward. That's why sometimes you have to ask yourself if you might be sitting in a bucket of crabs from which you must break free.

You might hear people say things like, "Oh, I remember when John and I started working together. He was really nice. We would hang out together and go have a couple of beers after work. But now he's just work, work, work. He's so motivated by money. What a big brownnoser. I feel sorry for people like John because they don't have any balance in their lives." The truth is that what John is really trying to do is to excel, to pull himself up out of the pot, to separate himself from the pack.

Surround yourself, both personally and professionally, with people who will say, "Challenge yourself—move forward and enrich your mind. Set a bigger goal. Don't settle for average or mediocre." It is easy to be average; what is hard is to be unique. If you find yourself in an environment that isn't uplifting, ask yourself if you are wallowing in a bucket of crabs.

Read Books

Books are the quietest and most constant of friends; they are the most accessible and wisest of counselors and the most potent of teachers.

—Charles W. Eliot

One of the best ways to expand your world is the classic way: Read a book. In fact, read lots of books, as many as you can. I know that sounds unrealistic for most people in this fast-paced world of careers, children, and television, but reading will give you an edge. Reading is one of the most undervalued resources in our country today. Being more knowledgeable and articulate than your competition will pay off in increased sales. Get a library card if you don't already have one. That alone will put you in the select group of Americans who take advantage of one of today's best education/entertainment values, because library books are available to the public free of charge. A colleague of mine, Jim Rohn, talks about the fact that less than 10 percent of the U.S. population owns library cards—and they're free!

When you first read a book, then see a movie, which one is better? The book is always better. Why? Because your imagination can bring the material to life better than Hollywood's top producers and directors. Reading has so many benefits. It enriches your mind, your vocabulary, your sentence structure, your creativity, and your thought processes. Everything about reading is good, and yet we usually claim not to have the time, or we read just business books. The most vibrant people we enjoy being around are those who are well read, who live life, and who experience things. Those are the individuals you want at your party. Why? Because when they talk, people listen.

Listen to Audiotapes/CDs

There are thousands of books available on audiotape and a few stores now even specialize in these terrific motivational tools. Tapes are also available at the library. You can often buy tapes for less than the price of the book, and they are great in the car when you are stuck in traffic. They are also available through mail order. The average sales executive spends anywhere from 10 to 12 hours a week in the car. If you just take, say, 10 hours a week, times 52 weeks a year, that is 520 hours a year in your car. That's a heck of a lot of time. Just take a small fraction of that time, say 10 or 20 percent, listening to professional development tapes. Instead of listening to that music CD one more time, pop in some professional development material or get one of the *New York Times* best sellers and pop it in so you can enrich your mind. Enrich your creativity. It makes a tremendous difference.

Read Newspapers, Journals, and Magazines

Subscribe to a newspaper and read it every day. It is important to stay informed so you can discuss with your clients what is happening in the world. Current events are ideal for developing analogies you can use in your presentations. Subscribe to your industry's leading trade magazine. Most executives read these cover to cover and base business decisions on the information they contain. Cut out articles that may be of general interest to your client. You've got to read newspapers, journals, and magazines. Why? Because that's where you get all the great stories and anecdotes and humor and drama that you can incorporate into your material. And it's so great in the middle of a presentation when you can say, "You know, I just read an article in the *Wall Street Journal* that said . . . " or "You know what? I just picked up a trade publication called the *Mortgage Originator,* and it said . . . " or "I was reading in *Psychology Today* about. . . ." It shows that you're really up on today's trends. These are the kinds of things that separate you from the masses because you're asking to be an extension of their transaction team.

Create Brainstorming Groups

Assume a leadership role and create a brainstorming group. Get together with the people in your company or industry and think of as many harms as you can to use in your presentations. Also include prospecting ideas that work and identify those that don't. There are thousands of ideas you can develop through your think tank.

Look for a Role Model

Finding a role model will make it much easier for you to achieve your goals. Such a person already has covered the territory you want to traverse. Having a ready-made map will save you untold time.

Attend Courses, Workshops, Seminars, and Conferences

Attend training courses on personal development. One of the things that always amuses me is when people say, "Gosh, Terri, we would love to send all of our people to one of your training programs, but what happens if we train all of our people and then they leave?" The better question might be, "What happens if you don't train them and they stay?" It's just something to think about.

On a personal note, I would like to appeal to you to take advantage of any opportunity to hear a speaker, even if it's not directly related to your business. One of the things I have just signed up to attend is called *The Amazing Lives and Experiences Series*. Approximately every six weeks they bring in a speaker who has an amazing story to tell. I'm not necessarily getting any direct content for my business, but I believe that good mental input equals good mental output, and the more positive, enriching, and thought-provoking ideas I put into my head, the more my life will become enriched, thought-provoking, and adventurous. For example, the first two speakers in this series were poet Maya Angelou and former Texas Governor Ann Richards, both of whom were very inspirational.

Watch TV and Movies and Go to Comedy Shows

One of the most frequently discussed topics of conversation is the latest hit movie. People talk about what was on television, but you can beat that if you attend a few comedy shows. These provide outstanding material for your presentations. A great way to get people's attention is with a good joke they haven't already heard. Comedians have great one-liners that will add a spark to your presentation and help make it memorable. Just make sure the material is appropriate for your audience.

If somebody says to you, "Hey, you guys want to hear a dumb joke?" What do we say? "Sure." We don't say, "No. If it's a dumb one, I don't want to hear it." That is because we want to be entertained. We want to hear a great storyteller.

Evaluate Other Speakers

Attend speeches and sales presentations delivered by your competition and other industry leaders. If they are good, they've probably spent much time and energy developing their skills. You can learn a lot through analyzing how they speak. There is nothing like a live performance to serve as a free training seminar. There is something about the human-to-human experience of hearing a speaker tell his or her story that can change you. I hear these powerful speakers and the professional part of me analyzes them from a speaker's perspective. The debater part of me analyzes their material from a content perspective.

Conduct Customer and Competitor Interviews

Conducting interviews with customers or competitors means that you go out and actively ask questions about areas of interest with which you should be familiar. It relates to the *Be-a-Spy Principle* (see Chapter 7).

Join Professional Associations or Committees

Don't be intimidated by those membership fees that associations charge; join anyway. The dinners and get-togethers are an excellent way to keep up both with the people and the issues relevant to your industry. Networking in these groups is also an excellent way to scout new job opportunities.

Find a Mentor

Someone you meet through professional associations might be interesting enough to invite to lunch or dinner. Such informal meetings can allow you the opportunity to speak in depth with a recognized leader in your field. The information you learn will be well worth the price of a meal. Sharing in the experiences of someone who knows the ropes can save you a great deal of time and money. I mentioned earlier the importance and significance of finding a mentor but I really want you to consider that *you really don't know what you don't know.* Remember that the first step in accomplishing your wildest dreams is to just get a mentor who's already done it. The path becomes so much clearer and easier to follow.

My question was, "What is it going to take for me to someday get a book on the *New York Times* bestseller list?" Well, it helps if you are famous. But how was I going to get famous? I needed to talk to someone who had written a business book, someone who had been able to parlay television and film appearances into getting their book on the *New York Times* list of bestsellers. Who had done that? I thought of Harvey Mackay and Don Martin. Harvey Mackay lives in Minneapolis, so I flew there to meet with him. And I now have been working with Don Martin for the last three years on several of my book projects.

You have to reach out to these people; they won't come to you. You set the parameters, then you do what they tell you to do. You start by offering your services. You can't walk up to somebody and say, "Will you be my mentor?" But you can walk up to someone and say, "I'm really impressed with the work that you've done; if there's anything I can ever do for you, research or any kind of project . . ."

I know an individual who once raked leaves for somebody who they wanted to be their mentor. And the biggest lesson that you have to learn about mentoring is humility. But in the long run, the pearls of wisdom that you obtain will be worth far more than anything you could ever imagine. What will be the cost of *not* seeking out a mentor? Achieving your goal will cost you more time and more money trying to figure out how to get where you want to go. And you will undoubtedly make more mistakes along the way, and get more frustrated than you need to be. You may want to consider reading *Mentoring: The Most Obvious Yet Overlooked Key to Achieving More in Life Than You Dreamed Possible*, which I co-wrote with my mentor, Floyd Wickman. It explains how to build and develop effective mentoring relationships.

If you follow through on even half of the suggestions listed in the 12 keys you will go a long way toward improving both your presentations and your personal knowledge. Development in both of these areas will help you to become a more successful sales professional. Apart from the confidence that comes from knowing yourself, there is also the confidence that comes from knowing your customers. Anticipating how your customers will react emotionally to your presentation will help you move them toward the close.

If you don't follow through on your creative ideas, someone else will pick them up and use them. When you get an idea of this sort, you should jump in with both feet, not just stick your toe in the water. Be daring, be fearless, and don't be afraid that somebody is going to criticize you or laugh at you. If your ego is not involved, no one can hurt you.

—Guru Rhh

Consider Emotional Factors that Sell

People are inherently emotional and motivated by positive emotion. Knowing how to uncover the emotional factors that will move your listeners can be another great asset in persuasive communication. Following is a list of factors, often employed in the field of advertising, which are highly effective in all sales presentations:

- Love of romance.
- Urge of quality.
- Comparison of value.
- Pride of possession.
- Joy of attractiveness.
- Thrill of enthusiasm.
- Pleasure of prestige.
- Security of durability.
- Charm of desirability.
- Elation of suitability.
- Virtue of efficiency.
- Relish of satisfaction.

Let me describe a few of these so you will recognize them when you see them and later be able to employ them in your presentations.

The love of romance is commonly the underlying theme for perfume ads and can be found driving certain travel advertisements. Advertisers use people's love of romance to sell just about anything that consumers find appealing.

The urge of quality also is seen in consumer advertising,

particularly for automobiles. American automobile manufacturers pride themselves on the luxury interiors they offer and want to make sure consumers believe the cars are as reliable as are their overseas counterparts.

Supermarkets are constantly asking shoppers to compare the value they get at one store with that of another. Stretching the homemaker's food dollar is a national priority and has great appeal as an advertising theme.

Builders and real estate companies use the pride people feel in home ownership to attract business.

Here are a few others that are commonly seen:

- Health clubs promoting the joy of attractiveness.
- Amusement parks selling the thrill of enthusiasm.
- European luxury automobiles selling the pleasure of prestige.
- Hand-tool manufacturers appealing to the security of durability.
- Travel companies and airlines promoting vacations and ski trips through the charm of desirability.
- A highly advertised men's clothier expressing the elation of suitability.
- Laptop computers, cellular phones, and software technology playing to the virtue of efficiency.
- Restaurants appealing to the relish of satisfaction in promoting specialty menu items.

If you employ even a few of these emotional factors in your presentation, you will be able to build a strong, credible, and entertaining case for your listeners or clients to take action based on what you are telling them. You will be able to communicate material your listeners are unfamiliar with in a way that they will remember it—and remember you.

Overview

- Mistake number 4 is providing inadequate support. You must incorporate strong evidence as well as entertaining and relevant material into the body of your presentation to bring it to life and make your case compelling.

- As a presenter, strong support of your arguments will dramatically impact your message and your credibility.
- Major speech/presentation supports include anecdotes, analogies, definitions, examples, statistics, testimonials, hypotheses, and rhetorical questions.
- To stimulate your creativity and enhance your uniqueness in your supporting material, review the 12 keys to developing a more creative sales imagination.
- It is important to recognize the emotional factors that help to move your listeners toward making a decision. Many of these factors can be easily identified in most television commercial or advertising campaigns.

Next: With a sufficient number of anecdotes, analogies, and examples, as well as other speech supports, your presentation should be credible and entertaining. In Chapter 6 we look at another mistake often committed by presenters—failing to close the sale.

Mistake Number 5:
Failing to Close the Sale

If there is something to gain and nothing to lose by asking, by all means—ask!

—W. Clement Stone

Despite tons of literature on various closing techniques that sales professionals can use to encourage prospects to buy, one of the biggest mistakes people make today is failing to close at the end of their presentations.

After giving a presentation that is not only informative but persuasive as well, why would we shoot ourselves in the foot by not closing? Perhaps it is because we mistake a conclusion for a close. A conclusion is a wrap-up, usually a summary—an end to what we have been discussing. A close employs the specific call to action. The close tells our listeners what we want them to do next with the information we have given them.

Few People Close

In my training workshops, we ask participants to deliver an entire sales presentation from start to finish. The overriding realization once we go through the playback on videotape is that many people do not close—they just wrap it up, and that's it. They never ask their listener or prospect to do anything, like buy their product or service, or work specifically with them, or even set up the next appointment time. This is exactly what *not* to do, but it is an extremely common problem and accounts for millions of dollars in lost sales every year.

The problem people have with closing relates to our tendency to be too informative rather than persuasive. If you don't build a strong enough case, then you are going to have problems getting your listeners to act. Perhaps you tried to close after giving merely an informative presentation and were unsuccessful. That may be because you didn't build a strong enough case in the first place. Based on what you have learned so far, let's assume your presentation is well constructed and persuasive. But having a great presentation isn't enough. You are still going to have to ask your listeners to *move forward*. Once you have built your case, you must ask them to take an action step.

Fear of Rejection

Our doubts are traitors and make us lose the good we oft might win by fearing to attempt.
—William Shakespeare

We might ask ourselves, "Why don't people ask for such an action step more often?" One of the leading reasons is that they fear rejection. The fear of rejection makes closing uncomfortable, so they just skip doing it. It feels like you are setting yourself up to take a fall. But all you really are asking for is a commitment from your listener. There is something about human nature where people may very well do what they are asked, but if it is a little uncomfortable, like parting with their hard-earned money, they likely won't do anything until they are asked.

The Close in Fund Raising

The need to close at the end of your presentation can be exemplified by a story from one of my students who used to work in the human resources department of a large aerospace company employing more than 50,000 people. It was Bill's job to implement the company's annual campaign for charitable donations. The point was to obtain authorization from the workers to deduct weekly contributions straight from their paychecks. The money was later distributed to United Way and other organizations that helped the less fortunate. Each year the company would produce an elaborate videotape to show the employees why they should contribute. The sessions were handled by supervisors in groups of 20 throughout company facilities.

The first year Bill went through all the work of producing the expensive videotape and had the supervisors answer questions afterward. The employees were later mailed a card to fill out if they wanted to contribute. Participation through that method was poor, and his boss did not give Bill any strokes in spite of his putting in a lot of effort. Later, the company's marketing director took Bill aside and gave him a little coaching: "Bill, you need to give the employees the enrollment cards immediately after they watch the video. Then ask them to sign it on the spot."

A light went on in Bill's brain. Next year he got the same assignment again. This time, however, he made sure supervisors all had the individual enrollment cards at the time the employees watched the video. He also gave supervisors a brief data sheet that instructed them to ask their employees to be sure to sign the card before leaving the conference room. This time, the results were impressive; a far larger percentage of employees signed up for charitable contributions than had done so in the entire history of the firm. Needless to say, Bill was rewarded with a nice bonus check.

The difference in results between the two years had nothing to do with the basic presentation. The videos, which contained much good information, were comparable both years. The supervisors were present in both cases to answer questions. The only difference was that the second year, the supervisors asked employees to take the next step—sign the card, and do it now. That was the close. The approach calling them to take action was influential with those individuals who were undecided about whether to participate. Not everyone signed the cards, but enough of the ones who were on the fence were convinced to make it a far more successful campaign. The result was that tens of thousands of dollars more went to charity that year than otherwise would have been raised. And it was a simple fix that took no additional resources from the company.

The Elevator Story

There is a story I tell in my seminars about a young man who goes back for his third job interview to meet the company vice president. After they talk for awhile, the VP asks the fellow if he has any questions before they wrap things up. The young man says, no, that he has a pretty good indication of what the job entails, and thanks the vice president for his time. Then he asks, "Do you know when you will make a final decision about hiring someone?" The vice president says that they want to think about it, and that he will hear back, one way or the other within two weeks.

The young man thanks him and walks out of the office. Once in the hallway, however, he starts to think about it and realizes he never actually asked the vice president if he could have the job. Knowing the importance of closing, he mentally berates himself and wishes he could walk back inside and give it one last try. He then makes a quick trip to use the telephone before coming back out to the hallway and summoning the elevator.

Suddenly he realizes that the man with his back to him who is standing directly in front of the elevator is the vice president who had just interviewed him. They exchange an awkward greeting and step into the elevator, both lunging for the button that indicates lobby.

The young man decides he isn't going to miss another opportunity. He looks the vice president in the eye and says, "You know sir, as I walked out of the interview, I thought to myself that the one thing I didn't tell you was how much I want this job." The young man uses the next 30 seconds to emphasize how much he truly wants the position, how much research he has done on the company, how many people he has talked with who respect the vice president. Finally, he says, "I would really like an opportunity to be a part of your team. When you are thinking about whom you are going to select, I really hope you will consider me, and more importantly, I want to let you know that I very much want this job."

The vice president, who might have taken offense, has exactly the opposite reaction. He looks at the young job candidate and smiles. "You know what, young man, because you asked for it you can have that job. I want you to report for work Monday morning at eight sharp, and I'll have the HR department process your paperwork. Welcome aboard." He then grabs the young man's hand, shakes it strongly, and walks off the elevator.

Meanwhile the young man is excited beyond belief. He walks off the elevator in a daze and looks up at the sky. "Thank you," he says. Then he starts congratulating himself: If he hadn't asked for the job, he wouldn't have been offered it. He was so lucky to get a ride down the elevator with the vice president. But was it all luck?

Know Where You Are Going

As a sales professional, you often will have to go through several presentations before you complete the sale. This is not unusual today when hundreds of thousands of dollars may be on the line. And as a job seeker, you might find that it is standard to have four, five, or even six interviews before you get hired in a decent position. There are usually a number of people who have to meet and approve of you before you can come aboard. In each interview, you should have a clear objective in mind of what is needed to take the next step in the process.

Most of us have walked out of a meeting or a job interview without closing—in other words we haven't obtained a commitment from the other party to move the process forward. In simple terms, we haven't asked for the business. Neither have we set up the next appointment time. In today's market, you rarely hear the word "no" anymore. What you hear is, "I'd like to think about it." When you hear that phrase, be on guard. You may be headed toward a no-sale situation. Next time you are giving a presentation, think of the young man in the elevator and how fortunate he was to have a second opportunity. Be sure to take advantage of the opportunity you have following your presentation and execute a good close—get a commitment in the form of a signed contract or set up the next appointment. Don't just conclude your remarks and expect your prospect to take the next step for you. Remember that you won't get what you don't ask for.

I'd Like to Think About It

In my live seminars people ask me, "Terri, what do you do when someone says, 'I'd like to think about it'?" No matter how good you sound, and no matter how persuasive your case is, you still are going to run into situations where people say, "I'd like to think about it." I will share with you what I do, but does it work every time? Nothing works everytime. But it is one more device you can put into your tool bag in case a situation like this comes up.

When I get to the close of a presentation and I ask them to make a commitment or move forward and they say, "You know what, Terri, I'd like to think about it." I say, "Okay, I understand this is a big decision and you may want to review some of the materials I've given you. I know you are very busy, so let's do this: Why don't we break out our calendars right now and set up the next appointment time when we get together. I'm sure that once you have had an opportunity to review the materials dealing with my experience and the agreement I've prepared for you, you probably are going to have several questions. I am sure I will be able to answer them for you at that point."

Why do I say this? The first reason is that we don't want to play stalker. (Maybe you can relate to this!) What I mean by *stalker* is that it is not uncommon that when we have tried to follow up with the client two, three, or perhaps even five or six days later (after having left them 5 or 10 unreturned messages) we don't want to call anymore. The reason is because we are starting to feel like a stalker! The temptation is to just let go of the prospect and assume the sale is dead.

You would be surprised how many times deals go awry or nothing happens because the sales professional just lets everything go. We just don't want to play stalker anymore because it feels uncomfortable. So to avoid this problem, I try to get the client's commitment to a calendar date right then and there. If they start to hesitate about setting up the next appointment time, I try to arrange it at a place that is very attractive for them—either a really nice restaurant (that they pick) or perhaps on the golf course. Now personally, I hate golf, but I took golf lessons anyway for one reason: business deals often are closed when the players are on the back nine. It is just another way I can meet with them and move the transaction forward.

Most of the time they are willing to set up the next appointment, and I don't have to play stalker. But if they still won't set up the next appointment, it typically results in revealing their real objection. If I can find out what that objection is, then I can deal with overcoming it. However, it's the vagueness contained in "I'd like to think about it" that creates our biggest problems.

Closing an Interoffice Presentation

The reluctance to close is seen throughout the business world with significant consequences. Sometimes even in interoffice meetings, when we are required to get together to discuss certain things that are happening, many of the meetings end up being informational. And there is work to be done! What's sad is that there frequently are no action steps as a result of the internal meeting. That is why it takes so much longer to get things done. A good recommendation would be that the close for an interoffice meeting is to ask: What are the action steps we must take? What do we want to happen next as a result of this meeting?

Whether you are in an interview and asking for a job, an interoffice presentation where you need to call for an action step as a result of the meeting, or a traditional sale with a potential prospect, the point is you have to close. When you do, you give your prospect more limited choices. They can say "no," they can say "yes," or they can say, "I'd like to think about it." If you hear the latter, you can move to set up the next appointment time.

If you happen to be in a retail sales environment and the customer says he or she isn't sure whether to move forward and make a purchase, you can offer to put the item on hold for 24 hours in exchange for his or her telephone number. You can offer to call the customer the next day after he or she has had a chance to discuss it at home with others.

The Guitar Salesman

I have a friend who has allowed me to share the following story but prefers to remain anonymous. So for the purpose of this story, we will call him Charlie. He is someone who was a frustrated guitar player. He took lessons when he was young, but his family split up and he moved out of town to a village where no guitar instructors were available to him. He never finished his lessons, but he always thought he would get back to it someday and always wondered what it would be like to be an accomplished guitar player. One day, years later, he had some time to kill while visiting Santa Monica, California, site of a huge guitar store.

He wandered inside to see what instruments were for sale and got talking to a knowledgeable young salesman, who sensed his deep need to own a good guitar. The store was temporarily out of stock of the blues guitars in the price range Charlie was interested in, so Charlie left. As he was heading out the door, the salesman asked for his phone number so he could let him know when the next shipment arrived. After arriving back home, Charlie forgot all about his spontaneous guitar shopping experience, but a couple of weeks later, he got a phone call from the salesman. The store just received a shipment of the exact type of guitar he and Charlie were discussing in the price range that Charlie wanted. Taken aback by the unexpected phone call, Charlie listened politely to the salesman and promised to come by the store in the near future. Of course he never found the time and again forgot about it.

The salesman didn't give up on Charlie, however, because he knew he really wanted a guitar. About a week later, he called a second time and talked to Charlie about how great the guitar sounded. It had a rich, deep tone, he said— far superior to anything in that price range that the store had carried in a while. He also told him that by now, he had only one left and that if Charlie could come by tomorrow, he would hold it for him. When he came in, he would set it up so Charlie could pay for it in three monthly installments with no interest charges.

Charlie was sold. He knew he wanted the guitar; he now knew he could afford it. The only obstacle was Charlie's wife, who was not big on discretionary purchases. His solution was to take his spouse with him to the guitar store, which just happened to be around the corner from one of West Los Angeles' finest Italian restaurants. Needless to say, Charlie now is the proud owner of a beautiful blues guitar. And one of these days, he's going to learn how to play it!

The point is that just because you can't close a prospect on the spot doesn't mean it is a dead prospect. While you can't spend all day on callbacks, you owe it to yourself and your customer to get beyond the "I'd-like-to-think-about-it" stage. You do that by closing.

Overview

- Mistake number 5 is failing to close the sale. Remember—most people conclude at the end of their presentations, but they don't close. There is a big difference!
- A conclusion is a wrap-up; your close is the specific call to action—what you want your listener to do as a result of your presentation.
- Fear of rejection is a common excuse for why people avoid closing at the end of their presentations. Remember—you don't get what you don't ask for, and your competitor will most likely ask if you don't.
- When faced with the response "I'd like to think about it," consider asking the prospect to set up a time for your next appointment.

Next: Closing at the end of your presentation will have a greater effect on your success than any other single change. However, keeping the attention of your audience is something many people have trouble with, so in the next chapter we turn to the mistake of being boring.

Mistake Number 6:
Being Boring, Boring, Boring

Perhaps the world's second worst crime is boredom. The first is being a bore.

—Cecil Beaton

Those deprived of sleep have learned of a new cure for insomnia: Just attend a colleague's business presentation! Most people give a presentation not intending to bore their audience to death—but they do it anyway.

People's presentations are replete with too many facts—the same old stories delivered in a flat, boring, monotone voice. Frankly, this is not going to capture your clients' attention or maintain their interest. A boring presentation is a waste of both yours and your clients' time and creates a poor image for you and your company. If you can't attract your clients' attention, you won't be able to connect with them. If you aren't communicating, nothing is going to happen.

One of the reasons people don't listen and retain information is that they are bored. We have to get people listening to us in order to maintain their attention. Every college student knows the professor who comes to class and reads the same flat lecture, from the same boring notes, in the same monotone voice, every semester. The result is students falling asleep. We must be interesting and entertaining if we want people to listen, and that means our presentations can't be boring.

The problem with boring presentations is somewhat obvious, yet people continue to give them over and over again—perhaps they don't know how they look and sound. Most professionals don't realize how truly boring their presentations are. When they are asked for self-evaluations after seeing themselves in a video playback during training, they say, "Well, maybe I went a little bit too long," or they might say, "Maybe it was a little bit boring."

I will return with, "So why did you keep going?"

They will say, "Well, I had to get through the material."

When you are practicing your presentation, ask yourself if your audience will find it interesting. If you hear a little internal voice saying, "I think this is boring," then it probably is. You must create a presentation that is worth listening to if you want your audience to stay attentive.

Somebody is boring me. I think it's me.

—Dylan Thomas

How many of us have had the experience of speaking with someone who didn't particularly want us there? When I raise this question in my seminars, it usually elicits laughter. Creating such situations is part of our job—right? Part of our responsibility as sales professionals is to meet with people who initially don't want us there. Our job is to turn them around and make them extremely pleased that they shared their time with us.

Audience/Customer Analysis: Be-a-Spy Principle

Preparation is the key to developing a powerful presentation. It goes without saying that you need to know your products cold. We will assume that if you are reading this book, you have passed that stage. Next you must decide who your customer is and determine why he or she should use your service. Then you must identify your competition. Finally you will need to know if your customer uses your competitor and, if so, why. You can find out this information by asking the right people. In fact, you can become a spy. I call it the *Be-a-Spy Principle*.

The first target of your intelligence work always is your audience. Who are they, what are their tastes, and how can you communicate with them? What stories and illustrations can you employ based on this information to make your presentation more interesting?

Following is a story I tell in my seminars that illustrates how rewarding it can be to know your customer-audience.

Leveraging Bass Fishing

One of my prospects for a seminar program was a gentleman whose personality was quite gruff and somewhat abrasive. However, I had approached him by following up on a referral that I had received from several of his sales managers. I had done all of the things I was supposed to do—I had sent the literature and made innumerable cold calls. However, he was protected by an efficient and effective secretary named Norma. I could never get past her. It was turning into one of those situations where you just figure it's easier to give up. (Let's face it, the average sales professional gives up after three attempts. The toughest transaction takes place after many more attempts, depending on the type of sale and the normal selling cycles for various products and services.)

Mistake Number 6: <u>Being Boring, Boring, Boring</u>

I had called the prospect many times, and it was Friday afternoon, so I thought, well, maybe I'll get lucky. "Diligence is the mother of good luck," as Benjamin Franklin once said. This must have been my eleventh attempt, and that's diligent enough for even the most stubborn prospect. So, I dialed his number, and to my surprise, he picked up the phone.

"Oh, Rick, hi, this is Terri Sjodin" (I was so shocked that he picked up the phone it took me a couple of seconds to re-group). "I have been trying to get in touch with you for a couple of weeks—I guess I was expecting to hear Norma's voice. How is it that you happened to have picked up the phone?"

He said, "Well, Norma is at lunch."

I said, "Well, she's great—anyway, I wanted to follow up with you—I sent you some materials, and the reason that I am calling is . . ."

I rolled out my whole set of mini-sales pitches that I use on the telephone. That is a very significant part of the job of sales professional—the telephone presentation. I was able to introduce myself and tell him why I wanted to meet with him, and reluctantly he agreed to get together with me the following Monday.

As I hung up the phone, I thought, what do I really know about this guy? Not very much. So I waited a couple hours, picked up the phone again, and called his secretary. I said, "Norma, this is Terri Sjodin. I have just set up an appointment with Rick for Monday morning. I always try to tailor my presentations to meet the needs of my clients, and I was hoping that you might be able to tell me a little about Rick."

And she said, "Well, uh, what is it that you want to know?"
I said, "Well, maybe just some of his hobbies or interests?"

She said, "The only thing I know is that he really likes to go bass fishing. I don't know if that helps, but that's all I really know—and I really have got to go because the phones are ringing off the hook here." With that she hung up.

My knowledge of the world of bass fishing is pretty limited. So I started flipping through my directory of knowledgeable individuals and came up with my father. I said, "Dad, what can you tell me about bass fishing?"

He said, "Bass fishing? Why in the world would you want to know about bass fishing?"

I said, "Well, I've got this client, and I'm trying to develop some rapport."

He said, "Terri, the only thing I know is that there is a TV show on Sunday called *Bass Masters*. Maybe if you watch this show you can pick up a few tips."

When he said there was a television show devoted to bass fishing, I almost started laughing—I simply couldn't believe it. I pulled out the *TV Guide*, and sure enough, there were two back-to-back *Bass Masters* shows on Sunday. Apparently there are a series of televised fishing shows hosted by Jimmy Houston, who is the Regis or Oprah of the fishing world. Jimmy invites guests from the sport-fishing world onto his show, and they discuss various fishing techniques and tackle setups.

I had no idea that bass was the big game of the fishing world. I didn't know that if you were a serious fisherman, you were called an angler. Nor did I know that there are all kinds of special bass tournaments for which you need to have a bass card. If you are beginning to wonder what this has to do with giving a sales presentation, the answer is absolutely everything!

Monday morning rolled around, and I walked into Rick's office, but he acted as though he never wanted to make that appointment with me.

What I heard: "Oh, Miss Sjodin, you know what? We are really pressed for time. I have a lot of things that have come up this morning. We are going to have to do this in about five minutes." (Has this ever happened to you?)

I just took a deep breath, walked into his office and said, "So, how was your weekend?"

He said, "Oh, it was fine, fine—very productive. I had a bunch of things I had to do around the house. Not really very exciting."

"You know, the same thing happened to me," I said. "I have been doing so much traveling that I haven't had any time to catch up on my laundry. I had this big pile of laundry that I had just pulled out of the dryer. I threw it on the living room floor and figured I would just kick back and fold some clothes while I watched TV."

Then I brought it up: "I understand that you enjoy bass fishing, so I started watching this show—I'm sure you heard of it—it was called *Bass Masters*."

He was stunned. His entire facial expression changed. He said, "You watched *Bass Masters*?"

"Yes," I said.

"This past Sunday?" he replied.

"Yes—it was a pretty good show," I said.

"Yea, good show—it was a double *Bass Masters* weekend!" he said, getting more animated.

"I know," I said. "I caught both episodes."

He thought it was just great that I had seen both these shows. Then he started telling me how it was his dream to someday go fishing with Jimmy Houston, and how he wanted to become a professional angler.

Suddenly he whips out his appointment book and says, "Young lady, have you ever been bass fishing?"

I said, "No, I haven't."

"Well, I'm taking my family, would you like to join us?"

"Are you kidding? I would love to go!"

Finally, after a few minutes, I said, "I know you are really pressed for time, but I do have a few ideas on how I might be of service to your organization."

He said, "Okay, hold on a minute." He then got up and closed the door, and I went back to my original 30 minutes. Not only did I complete the transaction but eventually arranged six additional programs to be presented to his organization.

The point of this story is to impress upon you how important it is to incorporate the personal, as well as professional, wants, needs, and expectations of your clients into the body of your presentation. If you already know this, then this is just a reminder of a technique that you may want to employ more often.

The secret is to be creative and put some energy into your presentation. This helps to make it more interesting to the client. It doesn't matter whether your creative ideas and homework are employed in the beginning, middle, or end of your talk, because it all contributes toward moving us away from the pitfall of being boring! To stay sharp, practice with a tape recorder and listen to the playback to determine where your presentation begins to fall apart. Then make improvements accordingly. Be sure to use material that is appropriate for the audience, whether presenting to one person or one thousand people.

If You Don't Want to Be a Spy, Ask for Information

Eventually, someone is going to catch you making inquiries about matters they may perceive to be outside the course of normal business. And what happens if you get caught? Should this happen, simply tell him, "Mr. Jones, you are absolutely right. You caught me! I was doing my homework, but I promise you this: I will put as much energy and effort into maintaining your business as I have put into obtaining your business from the word 'go.' I hope this is the kind of person you want working with you on your transactions." Do you think people are going to be upset when you come back with a response like this? Not at all, they want someone who is willing to hustle in order to get their business. This response works almost every time.

Finding out information about a customer or group of clients frequently requires only that you ask. Usually it takes just a couple of minutes. Before an appointment, I will call and say, "Ms. Jones, this is Terri Sjodin. I'm calling to follow up with you and confirm our appointment for three o'clock today. I'm trying to do some research so my presentation can meet your specific needs. May I ask you a few quick questions? They will take only about 10 minutes. If you help me, I can tailor my presentation to meet your specific requirements."

People usually agree and are even more interested in working with me because I am custom-tailoring my sales presentation to their individual circumstances. It often can even be another way to impress them with my service. The converse to this is to spend the first 10 minutes talking about something they already know. That is an unforgivable waste of your clients' time and very costly for you.

To customize your presentation for your clients, you must ask questions and also listen to what they say or what others say about them. You must become an active listener.

In Nido R. Qubein's book, *How to Be a Great Communicator*, he suggests the reason we pay little attention to developing our listening skills is that we take them for granted. To become better listeners we need to understand what listening is and to take a fresh look at this undervalued, but extremely important, sales activity.

Surely you know someone who is a particularly impressive listener. This person remembers things we say, asks insightful questions, and generally makes us feel good by leaving us with the impression of truly understanding—and therefore caring about—who we are. Unfortunately, most of the time we don't live up to that standard—nor do our clients.

Performing a Competitive Analysis

Listening to and learning about your client is vitally important, but so is learning about your competition. Once you know whom you are up against, you can figure out if your prospect uses their product or service.

The key question here is why do they use them? The answer will give you information about adapting your presentation to the client's needs. Let's face it: Everyone wants to know what the competition is doing. Football teams even watch each other's game videotapes so both sides can better prepare for upcoming games.

Identify the Competition

After spending time in any industry, you will begin to know your competition. If you call on someone who has just bought from another salesperson, say, "Oh really? Whom did you purchase it from?" Eventually there will be certain names that you hear repeatedly.

How Do You Measure Up?

Having a picture of the competition and a list of the firm's products and services, you begin your competitive analysis. That means you take a hard look at how you measure up in the marketplace. It is your responsibility to find out what makes your competitors unique and why they are getting sales that could be going to you.

Find out how your product is superior to that of your competition, and where theirs can beat yours, if at all. List your company's strengths and weaknesses. Develop a strategy to promote the former and minimize the latter. Figure out how best to offset the advantages held by your competitor. You may want to start doing a few of the things that have created a positive reputation for the other firm. Emulating your competitor's strengths may be necessary to improve your marketplace standing. Why reinvent the wheel?

Service: A Competitive Checklist

Despite the outcome of your competitive analysis, there is one area you can always control: service. Measure how accurate you are, how friendly you are, and whether you do follow-up work. You can completely control these areas, as well as your enthusiasm. They all count heavily (particularly your enthusiasm) in your client's decision whether to work with you or with someone else. Always share your personal enthusiasm or passion with the client regarding why you work in your chosen profession. Passion and enthusiasm are contagious and will make people want to work with you long term.

It's All In Your Delivery: Be Interesting and Entertaining

Controlling the way that you use the words in your talk is another way to avoid being boring. One of the exercises we routinely do during training is to videotape students telling a personal adventure story and then have them make a second, business-related presentation. The personal stories always are much more interesting, and it is not because of the subject matter. The difference is that when people tell their personal adventure stories they do it with enthusiasm. Students change their voice inflections, manipulate their facial expressions, contort their bodies for demonstration purposes, and are animated and entertaining. But something happens when they deliver their business presentations— they become boring!

After students see a video of their business talks, they often apologize for being boring. It almost goes without saying that if you think you are boring, there is a high probability your audience thinks so, too. The point to remember is that you should allow all the personal energy and enthusiasm you would normally share with your listener when telling a personal adventure story to come through in your professional presentations as well. Following are 10 tips to help prevent your presentations from slipping into the boring zone.

Tip Number 1:   Modulate Your Voice for Variation

One of the things that you can do to keep your presentations exciting is to maintain control over the sound of your voice. This is particularly relevant in selling because you should be in tune with your listener anyway. If someone is speaking softly to you, you match his or her tone and volume. Have you ever had the disconcerting experience of having a salesperson repeatedly speak loudly to you after each of your soft-spoken questions? Conversely, if your prospect is loud and aggressive, you need to be more assertive, yet still calm and pleasant.

Controlling the tone and volume of your voice allows you to make your talk sound more interesting while you stay in touch with your client. Being able to project your voice so that you can be heard is half the battle. Inexperienced speakers frequently don't talk loud enough for everyone in the room to understand them. The tone you use and your vocal variation allow you to project your own personality and to create a positive response whether you are speaking to one person or a large group of people.

Here are several exercises that will improve your tone and your ability to articulate.

1. Sing in the car and shower (with or without radio).
2. Pretend to speak with an accent (parlez-vous français?).
3. Practice your talk using different emotional tones, such as love or anger.

Above all, be aware of how you sound, and don't hesitate to use a standard tape recorder to practice your talk. How many of us were shocked the first time we heard our voice on our voice mail or phone recorder? We reacted by rerecording the message over and over—sometimes putting in more time on our outgoing voice mail messages than we do practicing our sales presentation. Take a tape recorder along on your next one-on-one sales call. If your presentation is boring on the tape, you need to spice it up. I assure you that you will catch deficiencies in your talk that you will want to fix. (Those missteps undoubtedly will act as incentives for you to put more preparation into your presentation.) A good book that goes into more detail on this subject is *PowerSpeak* by Dorothy Leeds. In it she talks about the many tools speakers have at their disposal to make their voice interesting. They include the following:

- *Volume*: Volume adds variety to whatever you say.
- *Pitch and inflection*: Different from volume, pitch and inflection reflect your overall tone.
- *Pace and rhythm*: How fast or slow you articulate the words and sounds.
- *Emphasis*: This affects your word and syllable stress. According to Leeds, "The key point is to be sure people get your main ideas. Help them by subverting the less important ones. A common fault of speakers is to emphasize too many things; you should isolate the key points you want to emphasize."
- *Attitude*: The same word or phrase can take on radically different meanings, depending on the attitude implicit in your voice.
- *The pause*: Powerful speakers use the pause several ways—for emphasis, effect, and mood. Pauses can be long, medium, short, or very short—as when you're just drawing a breath. They can also signal a transition.

Tip Number 2:   Good Diction and a Comprehensive Vocabulary Are Essential

---

Another helpful skill in keeping your audience's attention is the use of good diction. Diction relates to both your choice and use of words as well as to how clearly you pronounce them. Good diction is the mark of a well-educated person.

One way to improve your enunciation is to speak more slowly. Most people speak too quickly. One way to slow down is to practice reciting tongue twisters. They remind us of the need to enunciate and force us to slow to a crawl. Here are a few good ones:

Theophilus the thistle sifter
While sifting a sifter full of thistles

Thrust three thousand thistles
Through the thick of his thumb.

I stood on the steps of Burgesse's Fish Shop
Mimicking him hiccuping
And welcoming him in.

Silly Sally sits and shells her peas
All day long she sits and shells
And shells and sits
And sits and shells
And shells and sits.

Remember that in giving a talk, even if it is one-on-one, you are assuming the role of an authority. If you mispronounce words, use the wrong word for the intended meaning, and generally display a lack of knowledge, it is going to be difficult to maintain respect. However, everything is relative. The bumbling presentation before one group might sound like the message of a prophet to another. So don't withdraw just because you lack a formal education. Find an audience who appreciates what you have to say.

As you mature and become more knowledgeable, you will be able to impress increasingly sophisticated circles.

Tip Number 3:   Buy and Use a Dictionary

Your best friend in developing good vocabulary and diction is a dictionary. Buy two so you can keep one at the office. Better yet, get three—one for the car. Don't buy the cheap pocket type. They are good only for spelling. Invest in a hardbound collegiate dictionary that has multiple meanings. Whenever you hear a little voice in the back of your mind that questions whether you are using a word properly, spend the 60 seconds it takes to look it up. (If you can't even find the word, you are misspelling it and maybe butchering its pronunciation.) A best-selling book that has helped many people improve their vocabulary and diction and overall fluency with the language is *Thirty Days to a More Powerful Vocabulary* by Wilfred Funk and Norman Lewis. (It was actually required reading for me in my senior year as a speech communication major, and I am so thankful for it!)

Tip Number 4:   Have Fun with It and Keep 'em Laughing

Have you ever been to a comedy show to give yourself an attitude adjustment? You can do the same for your listeners.

> *Laughter is the shortest distance between two people.*
> —Victor Borge

Note your listeners' reactions as you proceed with your presentation. Try to keep them interested and enthusiastic. You want them happy that they spent their time with you. Have you ever been talking to a group when someone starts to fall asleep? It may not be because you are boring them, it may be because they were up all night for business or personal reasons. However, it is important that you try to rouse them. It is very impressive to clients if you can recapture their attention once they start to slip into oblivion.

Tip Number 5:   Emotional Conclusion

Conclude your presentation with an ending that emotionally drives home your point. Think of your speech support-stories, anecdotes, humor, think of how you can tie together everything you have been talking about, and think about your call to action.

Preparing for a presentation is similar to getting set for a ski race. Once you are out of the gate, there is no turning back. The pace is quick, the course is slippery, and all eyes are on you—the lone competitor barreling down the slope. And a sincere conclusion to your presentation will leave your listeners feeling good about the time they shared with you.

Tip Number 6:   The Warm-up

Before engaging in this type of competitive activity, you will need to do what all athletes do—a warm-up. It is important that you begin your presentation in a relaxed state. I always breathe deeply, close my eyes, and imagine how great my talk will be. I stretch and extend my arms and make circles with my out-stretched hands. I imagine applause at the conclusion of my speech or a smile on my clients' faces when they have signed the contract and made a commitment to the project.

I always try to eat a very light, nourishing breakfast the day of a big presentation. Frequently I practice with tongue twisters. If you remember to relax and warm up ahead of your talk, then things will go a lot smoother.

Tip Number 7:   Remember to Practice—Try a Full Dress Rehearsal at Home

Rehearsals are essential preparation for a good talk. Failure to rehearse says to the client, "I don't care if I waste your time." To prepare properly you have to run through a dress rehearsal at home. That means dressing up in the suit you plan to wear during your presentation and practicing every word.

Luck favors the mind that is prepared.
—Louis Pasteur

Turn on your tape recorder and practice your talk until it sounds smooth and convincing. Ask the people in your office to listen to your talk and critique it. Close your eyes and visualize delivering your speech. Imagine the positive response from the listeners. Practice all the words you plan to use so that you are familiar with each one and can say it without stumbling.

Tip Number 8:   Critique Your Presentations and Monitor Your Performance for Improvement

---

In order to improve, you will have to evaluate every presentation you deliver and identify its strengths and weaknesses. Be your own best critic and evaluate everything you do. Invite comments from others, and let them know that you are looking for criticism as well as the usual pats on the back. Sift through their comments to identify areas where you can improve. In Chapter 11, we will familiarize you with a Presentation Evaluation chart you can use.

Tip Number 9:   Gracefully Accept Criticism

When you are criticized more than you care to be, try to let some of it roll off your back. Don't let someone else's feedback break you. Gracefully accept compliments from others. In the long run, the best feedback will help prevent you from giving boring talks. And remember to find a role model, someone who does what you would like to do. The person should be very good at giving presentations and willing to spend a little time helping you. Perhaps you can return the favor by performing some helpful work for him or her.

Tip Number 10:   Employ Visual Aids to Stimulate and Enhance Your Message

---

We can't leave this section without touching on the role visual aids play in emphasizing your message. They help the audience to understand the points that you are making. They provide support to the body of your speech and can make your presentation more entertaining and engaging. The biggest problem, particularly for sales professionals, is that we tend to make visual aids the focus of our presentations. As a presenter, you need to remember that you are the star. The visual aids are the supporting players. They are there only to enhance your presentation—not to take it over.

With that being said, it is important to discuss the amazing benefits of visual aids. In his book, *Presentations Plus*, David Peoples points out the following:

- Your audience is 43 percent more likely to be persuaded with the use of visual aids.
- You can cover the same material in 25 to 40 percent less time.
- Learning is improved up to 200 percent for the listener.
- Retention for listeners is improved up to 38 percent.
- Typically the audience perceives the presenter as being more professional, persuasive, credible, interesting, and better prepared.

How Do You Determine When and Where to Employ Visual Aids?

It is important to ask yourself a couple of questions before you get started:

1. After looking over the Presentation Outline that you have created, ask yourself, "Where can I employ a couple of great visual aids to help clarify an idea or concept?" Hone in on the leading ideas that you want your audience to remember once the presentation is over.
2. Does your visual aid really add value and enhance your presentation? Or is it a text-based visual such as

words or bullet points? These are not true visual aids and may be serving the needs of the presenter more than those of the audience.

Overview

- Mistake Number 6 is being boring, boring, boring. Remember that it is the presenter's responsibility to build and deliver an interesting message.
- When you tailor your presentation to meet the individual personal and professional needs, desires, and expectations of your prospects, you can truly engage their attention and make a greater impact! Remember to do your homework in advance and then to get creative with the material.
- Learning about your competitors prior to delivering your next presentation can help you to better position yourself and your best selling points to your prospect. Remember to perform a competitive analysis, identify the competition, examine how you measure up, and establish a competitive checklist of where you can outperform your competitors.
- To help maintain an inspiring and entertaining delivery style, review the 10 tips to avoiding a boring presentation:
  1. Moderate your voice for variation.
  2. Employ good diction and a comprehensive vocabulary.
  3. Buy and use a dictionary.
  4. Have fun with your presentation and keep the audience laughing with you.
  5. Conclude your presentation with an ending that emotionally drives your point home.
  6. Warm up before your presentation.
  7. Practice enough and perform a full dress rehearsal the day before.
  8. Critique your presentations and monitor your performances for improvement.

9. Gracefully accept criticism and remember it can help you avoid the boring zone.
10. Employ visual aids to stimulate and enhance your message.

Next: In Chapter 8 we look at a very common problem that has been increasing with the use of laptop computers—relying too much on visual aids.

Mistake Number 7:
Relying Too Much on Visual Aids

A picture is indeed worth a thousand words. But it must be a good one!

—Dorothy Leeds

People who are going out to meet new prospects often become overly dependent on their brochures and printed materials. If handouts, brochures, and visual aids, including laptop presentations, could by themselves sell your product or service, it would be easy to sell and to promote your ideas. However, that is just a pleasant fantasy. You create the content. You create the magic in the message.

Visual aids can help the audience understand the points you are making. They provide support for the body of your presentation. The biggest problem, particularly for sales professionals, is that we tend to make the visual aid the focus of our presentation. As a presenter, you need to remember that you are the star, the visual aids are the supporting players. They are there only to enhance what you are saying, not to overpower your entire presentation.

Visual Aids as a Crutch

Whether using high-tech or low-tech support, many people use visual aids as a crutch to walk them through a presentation rather than to enhance and explain what they are telling their audience. For example, the high-tech hardware and software that computer companies have developed during the past few years has, in most cases, exceeded the skills of the people who buy it. Although we use these tools, we may not do so appropriately. The result is that we give up our role as entertaining, persuasive communicators to what we believe is a more interesting alternative—the computer-generated multimedia presentation. One of the things we should always keep in mind is that the tools at our disposal are subordinate to ourselves. If your visual aids ever upstage you, you have lost control of your presentation. This is when your presentation starts sounding like it's canned and headed for the boring zone.

What does the term *visual aid* really mean? Many people confuse the term and think it refers to a *medium*. Actually, a visual aid is something you can see, not the means by which you show it. For example, let's say you are a travel agent. You could make a bullet-point list of the amazing qualities of a vacation in the Bahamas including its:

- Beautiful ocean,
- Sandy beaches, and
- Palm trees.

The bullet chart is a form of visual aid, but it's really text—not a picture. For a better visual aid, you could show an actual photo of the sandy beaches and other amenities of the resort. The photograph is a true visual aid and communicates with the audience much more effectively than the bullet-point chart.

Other visual aids that can create a great impact in the minds of your audience include *pictures, cartoons, charts and graphs,* and *working demonstrations or models.*

What tools or media should I use to display my visual aids? To answer that, you should decide whether you want to adopt a high-tech or a low-tech approach.

High-Tech Visual Aids

High-tech visual aids are more complicated to operate and usually more expensive than low-tech aids. They include the following:

- *Laptop computer presentations* (displayed directly on your PC monitor or projected onto a larger screen).
- *Videotape and film.*

It is not only high-tech visual aids that people use improperly but low-tech aids as well. High-tech visual aids really are nothing more than low-tech aids taken to a new level. One of the questions that comes up frequently is, "How can I use visual aids or handouts more effectively in my presentation?" Just remember that you are the star, and your visual aids are the supporting players.

Low-Tech Visual Aids

Low-tech visual aids include the following:

- *Handouts and brochures* (fliers and other collateral material you distribute to your audience or prospect).
- *Flip charts* (individual boards with graphs or pictures that are sequenced—still used by many professionals).
- *Slides* (no longer considered high tech, this medium requires a projector and screen).

- *Overhead projectors* (my favorite because they still are the most versatile for small and medium-sized groups). Benefits of overheads include:
  1. You don't have to turn off the lights.
  2. It's easy to interact with the audience.
  3. You can easily mark up the transparencies if necessary.
  4. There are far fewer problems than with a laptop computer.
  5. They can be as simple or as elaborate as you want.
  6. They are cost effective.
  7. Most places have projectors.

  The disadvantage is that they are not suitable for larger groups of 100 or more because they become too difficult to read.
- *Working demonstrations and models* (this can be any kind of equipment from a computer running a certain type of software to handicrafts).

Example of How to Use Handouts for a One-on-One Presentation

Suppose I am meeting with a potential client in a one-on-one presentation, and I want to use a handout to help me sell my training and development products. I would extend the handout to my prospect, and say, "I just want to quickly show you this handout. Notice that this highlights our books and audiotapes and several of the different things that we promote at our programs to encourage continuing education and fulfillment at our events."

Why do I do it this way? For several reasons. First, when I extend the handout to my customer, I am inviting him to hold it. He automatically reaches out to grab it, which is normal, because when you extend a handout to someone you are inviting that person to accept it. However, I don't let go of the top of the handout! There are two reasons for this.

First, I stay in control of the visual aid. If I just leave the brochure in front of my listener, he is going to read it. That will take the attention away from me as the presenter and focus it instead on the visual aid.

Second, by holding onto the top, I can continue to make the point that I want. Then I can say, "What I want to do is take this from you right now, and I am going to put it over here in this file." Why? Because if I leave it in front of him, I know he is going to read it. But when I take it away, there is a tiny voice inside his head that says, "Hey! That's mine." (You always want what you can't have.) This example may exaggerate the point, but it does make the point of staying in control of your handouts.

When you use handouts in this way, you keep the focus on yourself. When you are finished with the handout, you have created a sense of urgency, and you have increased the odds that your listeners are going to read the materials that you leave behind with them.

Uncertainties of Computer Presentation Technologies

Visual aids are meant to explain and communicate what you can't say verbally. Many companies, in order to enhance their image to investors and customers, have standardized computer presentations. These generally are created with such programs as Microsoft PowerPoint and Lotus Freelance Graphics. Using these tools has its place, but as with all high-tech equipment, its use opens you up to the risk of problems you wouldn't face by relying on just your native oral skills to get the point across.

According to a leading Berkeley, California-based presentation systems vendor, a recent study found that as many as 60 percent of presentation problems are computer related. Even more surprising, almost half of the presenters polled do not carry backup materials for their computer-aided presentations.

Laptop Presentation in New York

I will never forget being hired to give a presentation for a large computer firm at a management briefing in New York. The company specifically requested that I give my presentation using a laptop so it would conform to their corporate style. I had a series of PowerPoint slides made that highlighted the points I wanted to get across in my talk.

One of my big concerns using computer equipment is that it might fail at a critical moment and interrupt my presentation. In the days when people used slide projectors, if the bulb burned out during the presentation, you would reach for the spare you had stashed away inside the projector and continue with your talk. Fixing a computer in the middle of a talk when you have 500 people sitting on the edges of their chairs waiting for your next slide is nothing less than a disaster waiting to happen.

Nevertheless, for this presentation, I created my slides on the computer and double-checked everything for accuracy. I made sure I arrived at the meeting room two hours before the event, did a sound check, made sure the connections were secure, and went upstairs to have a cup of coffee. The event started on time, but before I came on, another speaker, one who worked for the company, was scheduled to give his talk first. He plugged in his laptop and began his presentation. Right in the middle of his talk, the main system crashed. He bravely carried on saying, "I'll just give you the general outline—we don't need the visuals anyway!" Meanwhile, the meeting room was thrown into confusion, and the person in charge of audiovisuals was running around like the proverbial chicken with its head cut off. Five minutes later, they announced that the system was down for the duration of the morning, and they wouldn't be able to get it running for the rest of the meeting. The meeting planner turned to me with a pained look on her face and asked, "Terri—what are we going to do?" I reassured her that I could deliver the presentation with or without the visual aids.

To calm things down, the emcee decided to take a short break. In the meantime, the audiovisual technician got the system working after all. So I thought the problem was solved and plugged in my computer to begin my presentation, which was scheduled to run two full hours. Forty-five minutes into my talk, *wham*—the system crashed again—and this time really for good. However, as always, I made sure everyone in the audience already had a printed copy of my outline, so I just carried on with my presentation. Needless to say, my client was extremely impressed, as was everyone else. If you use computer technology in your presentations, you can be sure of one thing—sooner or later it's going to crash. When it does, if you are able to continue without a hitch, you can impress people even more than you would have done had it worked. It is not uncommon for me to retell this story at a seminar, and have countless individuals approach me at break and tell me similar incidents have happened to them! Obviously, it's a very common problem.

Given the uncertainties of computer presentation technology, my recommendation is to always present from an outline and recognize that your visual aids are just that—*aids*. Always ask yourself what you would do if your laptop presentation were to die in the middle of your talk. Be prepared to give your presentation without your laptop and practice doing so. And be sure to get there early to check your equipment!

Advantages of High-Tech Visual Aids

With my reservations clearly expressed about the challenges involved in using high-tech visual aids, I now can discuss the tremendous advantages these tools provide if employed by someone who knows how to use them. Many people believe that automated presentation tools are the future of sales and business in general. There is no question that it is a lot more professional to carry around a laptop and be able to transition from one product to the next than to show up on a sales call with armloads of binders stuffed with literature. For the person in a small business, it's not only what you say but also how you say it that counts. The style you use when presenting information is important to your success. Some will argue that slides and transparencies no longer hold viewers' attention in an era of video clips and personal computers. Going into a presentation with traditional overheads may give your audience the impression that you are somewhat out of date. PowerPoint and Freelance Graphics are not the only presentation tools out there, either. Adobe Persuasion, Astound Inc.'s Astound, and Micrografx Graphics Suite offer presenters a way to include animation, sound, and video in their presentations.

However, all of these new tools require specific training. Investing in the technology without having any training might be compared to buying a new car without a manual. Not knowing how to use laptop equipment properly in conjunction with your presentation can waste any money put into the new technology. Knowing the appropriate shortcuts as well as when to use the computer and when to close the lid in order to focus attention on the listener can be the difference between making or losing a sale.

Ten Simple Tips for a Successful Laptop Presentation

There are a number of pointers from industry experts that you should be aware of when creating a laptop presentation. I will summarize the most important ones.

1. Place your laptop—and yourself—not in the center of the screen but to the left. People read left to right, and your standing at the beginning of the slide will draw their eye back to where it is meant to be. Modify this rule as necessary for languages other than English.

2. Try standing under the light so people can see you; this will help you retain control of the presentation and make sure you retain your status as the star of the show. You may have to use a remote mouse and adjust the lighting.

3. Use body movements to direct people's attention. Motion toward the screen when you want your audience to look in that direction. Move around when you want people looking at you again. Use blank slides in between formatted slides so people pay attention to you instead of the screen. You can also close the laptop lid to focus people's attention on your one-on-one presentation.

4. Always have backup power including extra batteries.

5. Keep it simple. Use no more slides than you have to in order to make your point. Ask yourself if the slides you are displaying are necessary to build your persuasive case or are just another way to dump information.

6. If color is important, such as in a company logo, be sure to calibrate your computer with the projection screen on which your audience will see the image. Do this ahead of time so that you get what you want. Colors will vary from platform to platform, and when you introduce a new piece of hardware such as a projector you may get a different look.

7. Colors and special effects should be kept simple. The number of colors in each slide should be limited—usually no more than six. Don't distract the audience with overly fancy transitions and builds—use them to help your audience follow your meaning.

8. If your audience can't read what you are showing them, there is little point in trying. Stand back about six feet from the screen to test for readability.

9. Switch off energy-saving features and screen savers. These can interrupt your presentation without warning.

10. Become familiar with how to display your image at the same time on both the computer and projection screen. This is handled by a toggle switch, often a function key.

Be Afraid of the Dark

I had the opportunity to speak for a large health maintenance organization, and the company brought me in during the morning. Following my presentation they invited me to have lunch. Afterward, they were going to roll out their new millennium plan for all the employees. The room was already set up with two screens, and it was obvious they were going to show an elaborate multimedia presentation to kick off the new initiative.

After lunch, everybody filed into the room. The first thing they did was dim the lights. The projector went on, and everyone started watching the show. But what can happen to a room full of adults after a big lunch when you dim the lights? They get sleepy, of course. And what happened here when management finally turned the lights back on in the auditorium? It was almost like a room full of vampires at daybreak. Everyone was taken by surprise. How could they fall asleep so easily? The ironic part was that the company had spent thousands of dollars and vast amounts of time and effort putting together a multimedia show but no one had taken into consideration the timing after lunch.

It doesn't matter if the presentation has great music and dazzling visuals if you lose the attention of your audience by dimming the lights in the room. It's great to use computer technology and amazing multimedia tools, but remember: If possible, do not dim the lights in the room. Try to keep them on at full power whenever possible to ensure that you hold your audience.

LCD Projectors

One of the technical developments of the past few years that salespeople find helpful is the portable LCD projector. These projectors have come into their own with brighter colors and crisper images. Though the cost was fairly high a few years ago, it continues to fall as more and more people acquire them. These high-performance playback tools now represent a $1 billion-a-year industry. Much of that is driven by people in sales who want to take both a projector and a laptop with them on a sales call to avoid the kinds of problems described earlier. Having the equipment with you means you have more control over the results. Since there is less to go wrong, you are going to appear more organized and professional. These projectors are highly portable and weigh in at about six pounds, so they are handy to carry to meetings and trade shows. Some of the newer units are even designed to allow you to keep the lights on while you project your slides onto a screen or wall.

Electronic White Boards

For meetings where collaboration among participants is desired, an electronic white board may be just what the CEO ordered. These boards are similar to the traditional pen-and-ink white boards, but everything written or sketched onto them with their electronic markers can be downloaded to a PC.

Another display medium becoming increasingly popular is the big-screen TV—up to 40 inches—that some companies now use for showing computer-generated presentations.

Future Trends

It is becoming increasingly easy to create impressive presentations. Many software packages contain templates and simple tutorials that allow even a novice to quickly put together something that looks quite professional. Specialized graphics programs that can handle sound and video can make your small firm look like you are traveling in the big leagues. Using a high-quality color printer can add a fun dimension to your handouts that you can't achieve in basic black-and-white.

Software can be much more interactive than a conventional slide projector. Links can be embedded in most presentation and multimedia files so you can jump between slides at will to emphasize a point or answer a question from the audience.

The faster processing and larger hard drives found on today's computers, as well as CD ROM players and recorders, allow a presenter to play an entire multimedia presentation from a single CD ROM, which can also be duplicated for audience members or for later use.

The advances in technology can provide salespeople with powerful tools to enhance their messages and impress their audiences. But the best visuals in the world can't make up for someone who has no presentation skills. And if you have a poorly conceived presentation, it can make matters even worse. Relying too heavily on your slides can make you focus more on what you are saying rather than on how you are saying it, thus running the risk of overwhelming your listeners with facts rather than persuading them to act. You don't want your audience to get lost in the information. With these advanced technologies you can easily dump more information on people than they want or need. The answer lies in monitoring how much you are giving your audience and asking yourself if they really need all these facts. If they want more detail, they can always ask questions.

Practice, Practice, Practice; Avoid Possible Problems in Advance

It is critical that you practice your presentation using your visual aids ahead of time and that you plan for any unexpected problems that may arise. Ask yourself, "In the event my overhead projector dies, my video stops playing, my laptop crashes, my slide projector jams—what will I do to fix the problem quickly? How will I move on without it?"

Five Basic Rules Governing Visual Aids

Following are five rules or guidelines to remember that may prove helpful:

1. Don't use too many visual aids. If you do, they might lose their impact and bore your audience.
2. Stand to the side of what you are showing, not in front of it. Maintain your focus on the audience; don't talk to your visual aids but speak directly to the audience.
3. Keep it simple and easy to understand. If you are using numbers and words on a visual, make them large and easy to read.
4. Color can enhance your visual aids when it is pleasing to the eye and can add emphasis to a point. Use it to spice up an otherwise flat and boring graph. Just don't overdo it.
5. Think about the *wow* factor. That is, does it make people say "wow"? Get creative and do something fun and engaging.

Overview

- Mistake Number 7 is overreliance on visual aids. These tools can provide amazingly positive results for your presentations when employed effectively. Many sales professionals, however, use them as a crutch. Remember that you are the star, and the visual aids are the supporting players.
- The numerous options for your visual aids include charts, graphs, photographs, cartoons, demonstration models, and samples.
- Visual aids can be employed by using low-tech or high-tech media, including handouts, flip charts, slides, overheads, and computers.
- When employing high-tech visual aids in your presentations, remember the 10 simple tips to a successful laptop presentation.

- Memorize and follow the five basic rules governing visual aids.

Next: High-tech visual aids can be impressive to your clients, but only if you use them wisely. A boring presentation is still boring no matter how many PowerPoint slides you have. Giving an impressive presentation means that you are the star. In the next chapter, we discuss how you can keep control of your presentation by avoiding a common mistake—distracting gestures and body language.

9

Mistake Number 8:
Distracting Gestures and Body Language

Nobody realizes that some people expend tremendous energy merely to be normal.

—Albert Camus

We spent the last several chapters analyzing how to put together the parts of a powerful presentation. It is a technical job, much like assembling the sections of an airplane. Now in the cockpit, you may suddenly begin to get a little nervous as you start rolling down the runway. But that is what it is all about. We have just constructed a great flying machine. Now it is time to see how it takes to the air.

People get a great sense of exhilaration from giving a talk. They get a sense of exhilaration from making a sale. Both are competitive activities, and all the rules that apply to competitive sports apply to giving a powerful sales presentation. You can drag along making a sale once every 8 or

10 presentations, but, even if you can pay your bills that way (which is doubtful), can you handle that much rejection?

In order to create a strong presence you will need to communicate on both a nonverbal as well as a verbal level. We already have discussed how you will put together the words. Let's take a look at the other messages the audience will receive.

Body Language

Body language is *very* important to the sales professional and to anyone who is giving a speech. The way you move does three things: it conveys meaning, it influences the audience's attention, and it establishes spatial relationships. Your body naturally wants to gesture. For example, many people gesture with their hands while talking on the telephone. Do you ever cross your arms? That is supposed to mean that you are closed off and not receptive. It isn't always true, but what if your client has heard that myth and then sees you crossing your arms? Be certain the movements you use while giving a presentation complement your message and don't detract from it. Negative body language is typically a result of nervousness or lack of preparation.

Strange Things People Do

One of the things we do at Sjodin Communications is to videotape professionals during role-playing sessions, and then do playbacks. That way, people can see and hear themselves as their clients do. This area of training is where we have the most fun, yet it makes people uncomfortable and afraid of putting their presentations on videotape. Their attitude seems to be, "What we don't know won't hurt us." But the way the entire presentation comes across depends on our mastery of this final component. It is the art in the delivery. Your eye contact, body language, and the way you position yourself all comprise the finished product. What we try to do is to give people an opportunity to learn through the mistakes of others.

One of the things that we find is that if people don't learn to control their energy and adrenaline, it will come out in strange and incredible ways. The most important thing that you need to remember is that *your body naturally wants to gesture*. To prove my point, haven't we all seen someone involved in the previously mentioned activity of talking on the telephone while her hands are gesturing? Obviously, nobody can see her. She is not thinking to herself, "I am going to put my hand here first and over here next"—her body just naturally does it. Now, in the course of a presentation, when all of this adrenaline is running through your body, the energy has to go somewhere. The most normal outlet is in your body language. The following are a few of the unusual things people have done during their presentations when not channeling this energy effectively.

Hands in Your Pockets

Each gender has its own peculiar habits. Men have a tendency to speak with their hands in their pockets. You may not think that is a big problem except that all this energy has to come out somewhere. So they begin to do what we call the "chicken," in which their arms start flapping back and forth. Now if their collar or shirt is a little tight, it will look very strange because they begin to display almost a rooster effect when they start to move. My personal favorite is the gentleman who has a tendency to play with his keys or fiddle with his change. After a while, you begin to wonder what the heck it is that he's doing down there.

But actually, ladies are just as bad. Women are constant groomers. They have a tendency to incessantly touch their hair and their clothes or fiddle with their skirts. And women typically appear to have more nervous energy than men do.

One, Two, Three-Kick!

One of our students must have been a cheerleader in high school because every time she made a point, she kicked her leg out. Her name was Jamie, and whenever she would give an important presentation and had to make a point, she would kick out her leg. And I would say, "Jamie, we really need to watch that leg." She would look surprised and say, "I don't even know what you are talking about!" Suddenly, *whack*, that leg would kick right out again. So to tease her a little during the video playback, and help her become aware of her habit, we hit the fast-forward button. She looked as though she were doing the cancan. But the best part was that as she continued with the exercise, you could see her really trying to hold back that leg after she became aware of it.

We also have what we call the "jail stance" or the "parade rest," where people stand with their hands locked behind their backs. It seems like their hands are struggling to get away. We also have what we call the "fig leaf," because sometimes the person stands with hands cupped in front as if they are Adam or Eve in the Garden of Eden.

Pens in Pocket

We have other people who have a tendency to gesture with distracting objects or items. We often see individuals speaking with a pen in their hands. Whether it is a diamond-studded presentation model or a cheap plastic throwaway, a pen is very distracting. After a while, people aren't really listening to what you are saying: they are focusing on the pen. We worked with one gentleman, a very sweet man, whose name was James. He would speak with his pen and then he would rest his pen in his pen holder—which was his ear. Literally, on tape, I have a man with a pen, sticking out the side of his head. And as he is watching the playback, he is saying, "I cannot believe I do that!" A few seconds later, *whack* we watch as the pen goes right back in again. He was totally unaware that he was doing it. I worked with another gentleman who also spoke with a pen in his hand, and he would rest it in his tie. He would roll it up in his tie, and he would roll it down in his tie. He would roll it up in his tie, and he would roll it down in his tie. Finally, we took the pen away and he had this little dip in his tie where he had been rolling it. But my absolute favorite story comes from a colleague of mine, Ed Reilly, who had a gentleman in his group who was so nervous that he fiddled with the buttons on his shirt. He would repeatedly unbutton his shirt and then button it back up again.

Hands Near Your Face

One of our students told a story to the class about having a bee fly into his ear. He illustrated the point by sticking his finger right where the bee flew in. This could have been effective if done once. But throughout his talk he kept repeating the demonstration until it appeared compulsive. No matter how many times I interrupted and told him to stop doing it, that little finger would arch back up into his ear. Apparently he felt more comfortable with his finger sticking into the side of his head than he did with it resting at his side—at least when recounting his bee story.

Are You a Penguin?

Another favorite mannerism is doing what I call the "penguin." That is when a person keeps his arms straight down at his sides but flips his fingers up and out in unison. Presumably, he is trying to keep himself from moving, but the urge isn't completely suppressed. Others do what I call the "spider." That is when the fingers curl into a ball, then slowly fan out in an expression of extreme tension. Both gestures are terribly distracting.

The Robot

The robot often shows up on video. This is the person who moves around in a very stiff way as though all his joints need lubricating—sort of like the Tin Man after the rainstorm in *The Wizard of Oz*.

And though we might be laughing through all of this, what does it really tell us? It tells us that most of the time we are not aware of the body language, gesturing, and strange habits that we are using when we are giving a presentation. Everything from your posture to your body language, to the way that you speak, to your facial expression, to your use of visual aids comes into play. All these things either enhance or detract from your presentation.

Oops! Too Close

Spatial relationships are important to people. It is up to the sales professional to allow the client to set the speaking distance. This guideline applies most definitely in one-on-one situations. If the client invites you closer, then move forward. Make sure you test your spatial parameters with your client, however. Have you ever had a salesperson act too friendly from the start? That can be more offensive than someone who acts a little more distant.

Angry? Me?

Sometimes a person's facial expressions become contorted when they are giving a presentation. A man's eyebrows may come together, making him look very stern. While some people may interpret this expression as authoritative, others will see it as intimidating.

Try practicing smiling at the beginning and end of your presentation. It doesn't have to be a cheesy, fake smile, just that little human element. Your smile is a great asset. When you begin adding those personal stories and your particular brand of passion to your presentation, a smile will come naturally.

Eye Contact

Eye contact is very important to your listeners. Look directly into the eyes of your client frequently before looking away. If you are addressing a group, look into the eyes of individual members of the audience. It gives the others the feeling you are connecting with everyone in the room. If you are looking over the heads of people in the audience, you won't have eye contact.

Move with Meaning

Remember that your movements convey meaning. There is a big difference between moving with intent and pacing back and forth. Don't be a Dancing Dan, jumping all over the stage. Try shifting your weight at the precise moment you make the change to the next major point in your presentation. Try taking a few steps to the side as you approach a transition or new topic. The audience automatically will refocus its attention and understand, through your movements, that you are moving to a new idea.

Make a Commitment

If you want to be a good presenter, you have to get control of your distracting gestures and body language. Until you do, you will have little real impact on your audience. At this point, you need to consider how serious you are about giving a good presentation. If you are serious, I would ask that you make a commitment to get your presentation videotaped at least once a year. Do a role-play and get it on video so that you can see and hear yourself as your clients do.

Though most of the tips in this book can be adopted through simply reading about them, learning what distracting gestures and body movements you are making needs a perspective you don't have. Having a friend or spouse watch you and critique how poised you are works fairly well, but the best way to achieve the polish we all want is by watching a videotape of ourselves as we deliver the presentation.

The benefit of seeing yourself as others do can't be overemphasized. I was in Palm Springs on vacation once and decided to practice my tennis. Whenever I served, I got the ball in, but I just didn't feel good about my form. In fact, I felt very self-conscious about it because I thought that it looked ugly since it felt awkward. The solution, of course, was to take a lesson. The instructor used a videotape to show his students what they were doing wrong. After 10 minutes of serving and watching the playback with the instructor's comments, I knew exactly what was wrong and could correct it.

If you don't have a camcorder, you can rent one and then try doing a self-evaluation with the Presentation Evaluation Chart included in Chapter 11. You should be able to personally correct most problems after performing your speech evaluation. If you are a manager and are worried about how to evaluate fellow employees, I strongly recommend doing it on video since seeing yourself, even with all the flaws, is a more positive experience than an outside critique.

To get good, don't hesitate to seek the help of a professional such as a speech/debate coach at your local college campus or seek out a professional public speaking trainer. Also consider using the training and development resources within your company or an outside provider service.

Remember that it is not only what you say and how you say it, but also how you look and what you do with your body that communicates messages to your audience. In order to achieve the effect you want—a persuasive presentation—you need to be in control of the message. If part of the message is how you move, you need to be in control of your body at all times during your presentation.

Overview

- Mistake Number 8 is distracting and annoying body language and gesturing, which detracts from your presentation and impacts your credibility as a competent speaker.

- The way you move when presenting conveys meaning, influences the audience's attention, and establishes spatial relationships.
- Most negative body language is a result of nervousness and lack of preparation.
- It is not uncommon for individuals to catch themselves engaged in some pretty strange habits that they are unaware of when they speak—from hands-in-their-pockets to kicking out a leg or moving like a robot.
- To monitor and control our body language and gesturing habits we must first get our presentation on videotape and watch the playback, then make the appropriate adjustments.

Next: A complementary issue to inappropriate body movements is inappropriate dress. In Chapter 10 we look at ways to enhance your credibility through dressing appropriately.

Mistake Number 9:
Wearing Inappropriate Dress

If you want to make it on Wall Street or Main Street, pay careful attention to the clothes you wear and the visual impact you have on others.

—Nido R. Qubein

It's natural for everyone to think that the way they dress is absolutely fine, all the time, whether or not they know anything about clothes. Unfortunately, dressing for most people is a habit, and many of us just throw on clothes without much thought behind the impression we will make on other people. As long as we don't wear shorts to work and a tuxedo to the company picnic, we assume no one will notice, or even care. This is a big mistake, and one that many people today make repeatedly, particularly if you deal with the public on a regular basis.

The worst sins of inappropriate dress, of course, include those your mother reminded you about when you were growing up: disheveled-looking clothes that look like you slept in them, unpressed suits with no creases in the trousers, colors that are not coordinated, clothes that are grossly out of style, shoes that are inappropriate for your activity—the wrong style or color—or shoes that are scuffed up and worn down at the heels, ties that are too wide, or wearing too many accessories.

Most of us have been guilty of showing up somewhere, at one time or another, exhibiting one of these disturbing flaws! No, this won't do if you want to get ahead in your career (and these days, maybe even stay up to where you already are). Wearing inappropriate dress will definitely have an impact on people you meet for the first time, and I guarantee it won't be positive. When giving a presentation, it will negatively affect your audience, particularly if you are following someone else who happens to be well dressed.

Testing Your Credibility

To be in control of your presentations, you must be aware of the importance of how you dress. When your clients ask themselves how credible you really are, the first thing they look at is how you are dressed. When you walk through the door, people immediately begin to evaluate your professional credibility based on your dress. Does what you're wearing make a strong enough impression?

There is a discrepancy between how professional employees dress and how their supervisors think they should dress—I know because I hear about it in my seminars. Managers know that customers immediately begin to evaluate your professional credibility within a very short period of time based on how you dress. They are reluctant to say anything to their employees about inappropriate dress, however, and this is where one of the problems arises. Managers think the subject is almost taboo—too personal. Yet even though they are dissatisfied with how their employees look, managers don't necessarily want employees to feel pressured into having to spend money on clothes.

Is Your Success on the Line?

Michael E. Gerber, author of *The E Myth*, suggests that the color of your suit can have a tremendous impact on the success of your sales presentations. He suggests sales professionals try the following test for six weeks:

> For the first three weeks wear a brown suit to work, a starched tan shirt, a brown tie (for men), and well-polished brown shoes. Make certain that all the elements of your suit are clean and well pressed. For the following three weeks wear a navy blue suit, a good, starched white shirt, a tie with red in it (a pin, a scarf, or a necklace with red in it for women), and highly polished black shoes.
>
> The result will be dramatic: Sales will go up during the second three-week period! Why? Because, as our clients have consistently discovered, blue suits outsell brown suits! *And it doesn't matter who is in them*!

Does that mean that you should wear navy blue everyday? No, but it is something to consider if you're looking to put the finishing touches on your presentation.

Expensive clothes aren't essential. More important is that your clothes look clean, pressed, and coordinated in color and style. Obviously, you don't want to look disheveled, though it's surprising how many so-called professionals do. Our image should be appropriate to our message. In Corporate America, that frequently means conservative. Of course, it is also appropriate to consider adapting your dress to the people you are addressing; your industry may respond better when you don't overdress but rather display a style similar to your listeners.

First Impressions

For the same reason that it is important to dress appropriately, it is also critical that you create a positive first impression. People frequently judge us on things that have absolutely nothing to do with our professional ability. The very first characteristic they evaluate is dress. In addition to your appearance, your opening remarks will be what people use to form their initial, and often lasting, impressions. Roger Ailes and John Kraushar, in their book, *You Are The Message*, note that research indicates that we begin to make up our minds about other people within seven seconds of first meeting them.

People often draw conclusions long before we ever have a chance to prove ourselves professionally. In our unscientific polling of cold calls, we find prospective clients give salespeople an average of about a minute, and sometimes less, to create a positive first impression. During role-play drills in our workshops, we find that, if you are giving a one-on-one presentation to a man/woman team, you have just over five minutes to generate an overall sense of credibility.

We always want to walk through the door looking and feeling like a million dollars. The general manager of a Richmond, Virginia, men's and women's apparel shop was recently quoted in the Richmond *Times Dispatch* as saying, "To be perfectly frank, your clothes give a first impression when you walk in the door, and that is all that is saying anything about you until you open your mouth."

Gender Differences

Are there differences in what men and women notice about one another, in terms of dress? The answer is, yes. Men have a tendency to notice your tie first, then your shoes. They look to see if you have a dimple in the base of your tie, and they look to see if your shoes are sharp looking and polished. What do women notice? Actually, everything. And women have a tendency to be much more critical of one another than they are of men.

Does what you wear make you feel like a million dollars when you walk out the door? Steven A. Kelley, vice president of the human resources consulting firm Career Management Group Inc., believes there are three things to consider when choosing your attire for a job interview. You want to look good; you want to be comfortable and feel self-confident; and, you want to show respect to the person with whom you are interviewing—so you don't want to over- or underdress.

The old saying that "clothes make the man"—applicable of course to women too—is as true today as it was years ago. Some people say what you wear to an interview or business meeting is just as important as your qualifications.

Suits for Self-Confidence

To show how much dress affects not only what other people think about us but also our own attitudes during a presentation or interview, we need only look at the results achieved by the national nonprofit group that provides suits to low-income women seeking employment—Dress for Success. The women get two suits, one for the interview and the other for after they start work. Companies ranging from shoe stores to cosmetics retailers help with donated products.

Featured on ABC television's *Primetime Live*, Dress for Success women who received the free suits expressed tremendous boosts in their self-confidence when they were dressed properly for a job interview. Nancy Lublin, the founder of Dress for Success New York, was quoted as saying that her clients' confident attitude was a far cry from the nervousness they exhibited when they first walked into the agency. "They walk out of here really cocky and confident, and that's the point," Lublin said. The principle holds true for those seeking a promotion—if you look like you are ready to play the game you very well may be approached for a new opportunity.

Women's business fashions offer a much larger variety of choices than men's, and the proper length of a woman's skirt often is dictated by her field of business. According to one womenswear storeowner, "If it is a job as a decorator or an artist, you can go for a little shorter skirt. . . . But when you are in bookkeeping or a more professional/corporate job, you want to be a little more refined." It is okay for suit jackets to be short, and fingernails should be also. Long nails are not good during a job interview, she suggests, but hands need to look immaculate. Store managers say people seeking jobs in advertising, marketing, and retail can dress a little less conservatively than those in law or banking.

The Importance of Proper Fit

One vice president of a ladies' apparel shop in the South commented in the newspaper recently on the importance of a job applicant's clothes fitting properly. The comment suggests that getting to know a good tailor in your area is a wise move. "Before you even think about fashion, you should focus on having an outfit that is well fitted," said the executive in a media interview. "Regardless of your style, it makes a great impression—or a poor impression if poorly fitted."

You Never Know . . .

Some business people believe it is important to maintain a consistent and conservative image, even at play. In *Trump: The Art of the Deal*, Donald Trump says he is always dressed for business when he goes out because he never knows whom he might run into. It is something to think about. The day you go out with your hair in curlers or wearing an undershirt is the day Murphy's Law will come into play—if something can go wrong, it will go wrong. In this case, if someone like an important decision-maker can be where you least expect this person to be when you look your worst, she will be.

The Bachelorette Party

Once I shocked a small but important group of clients by appearing in a too-hip outfit at a local nightclub. It was a girlfriend's bachelorette party, and several of us decided we were going to paint the town. We all put on miniskirts and teased our hair so it stood up high. I wore black stockings, black pump shoes, and a black leather jacket.

We rented a limousine, and the five of us whisked off to the first of a series of nightspots. I was just getting into the mood of the place—which means I was mentally in "fun mode" on top of a dance platform—when I looked down and saw a table full of my business clients. They had been in one of my training seminars the previous week. They all looked shocked. Needless to say, they could hardly wait until Monday morning to report the incident to their manager. By the time I arrived at my office, I had a half dozen messages on my answering machine from my clients either chiding or teasing me.

Though I was on my own time that evening and just having fun, the incident made me acutely aware of how important dress can be to your business associates—and your career. You never know whom you might run into!

Dress Varies with Industry

A mentor once told me, "Terri, when it comes to business presentations, dress for what you aspire to, not for the position you currently hold." Most people have either read about or heard about the book, *Dress for Success* by John T. Molloy. What I notice most since his famous book was published is that some of the rules have changed. People today are required to dress differently depending on the industry in which they work and the particular event being sponsored. For example, a building contractor would dress differently from the CEO of a Fortune 500 company. And on Fridays, for most companies in the United States, it's dress-casual day—people are in sport clothes and look ready to play golf. Unfortunately, the tendency today toward dressing down—exemplified by casual Friday, has gone overboard, in my opinion, and may impair the image of the organizations sponsoring a more relaxed working environment for employees.

Grandmother's Rule

My personal rule of thumb always has been to keep in mind what I think my grandmother, Doris Burns, would say about what I am wearing. My grandmother is British and very polished. I always imagine myself going to meet her wearing something very conservative and very polished that would make her proud. It's the same image I keep in mind when I go to meet my clients. I want them to know that I dressed up in order to show them the honor and respect due them for the time they are willing to spend with me.

Dressing appropriately for every situation is a talent only a small group of individuals possess, but we should always *try* to look our best within the limits of our budget. A small investment in how you dress can pay big dividends in the business world.

Let's Go First Class!

How you look clearly does make a difference in a wide variety of circumstances. Often you will get better parking, better seating in a restaurant, and better service in retail stores. If you look like a million dollars, you will be treated accordingly. As a professional speaker, I travel all over the country and do so frequently. Normally, my clients pay for the tickets, and it is generally coach. I usually try to get upgraded to first class, however, through using mileage points, but sometimes I'm out of vouchers. In these situations, I will often go to the first-class counter and tell the ticket agent that I am a Gold Club member, but I'm out of vouchers. When I try this, I make absolutely sure that I'm dressed like a first-class passenger! Because I look good—*like a first class passenger should*—very often the agent will upgrade me despite the fact I don't have the necessary vouchers. It works only if I'm dressed appropriately. I tried it once wearing blue jeans and a sweater when leaving on vacation, and I was quickly denied.

Clothing Consultant to the Rescue

We have learned some valuable information recently about wearing inappropriate dress—one thing is that many of the industry books on dressing for success are slightly outdated. I strongly recommend that people serious about their careers meet with either a private clothing consultant or one who works for a major department store. The latter, in most cases, is free. You can get advice pertaining to color, style, and, most importantly, protocol for your dress requirements for varying presentations and situations. If no one is available in your area, consult Molloy's industry bible, *Dress for Success*. It can provide a basic guideline for you. My best suggestion, however, is to hire a professional clothing consultant.

Tips for Good Dress

Here are a few tips to keep in mind for dressing for success:

1. Look good, and dress appropriately for the type of meeting you are attending. There is a fine line between overdressing and underdressing, so get to know the culture from which your audience will be drawn.
2. Be comfortable, and look neat enough so as to feel self-confident.
3. Make sure everything fits properly. Get to know a good tailor or dressmaker. Whether the clothes are new or old, they simply must fit well.
4. Colors need to be coordinated. If you don't know the rules, do some further research on what goes together. Here's where a clothing consultant is invaluable.
5. Shoes should be clean and polished. Accessories need to be tasteful and should complement your clothes. Don't overdo it.
6. Clothes should let people know you are aware of what is currently in fashion without looking like a page out of a magazine.

Cost of Dressing Well

Yes, dressing well does represent a financial investment, but it is one that will pay you back many times over. It may cost you a little to upgrade your wardrobe, but it's an investment in yourself and your career. Some people spend thousands every year to look good. You can too if you want to, but you don't have to spend a lot of money on clothes to look neat, professional, and attractive. There are discount stores in business today that sell clothes for practically less than what it costs to make them overseas. I also know people who dress extremely well without ever buying anything new. Have you seen the high-end consignment stores that are popping up lately? Yes, you will have to shop around a little, but it is not hard to find bargains.

If you have a special event where a lot of decision-makers will be present and you don't want to buy an expensive outfit—borrow one from a friend or relative. They might be happy to lend you a blouse, shirt, or tie. You are only going to wear it once anyway, and, who knows, it may deepen your friendship. Just remember to give it back to him or her after the obligatory trip to a reputable cleaner!

Dress so that every single day you walk out of the house, you're dressed like a million bucks and you feel like a million bucks.

Overview

- Mistake Number 9 is wearing inappropriate dress. The way you dress for a meeting or presentation will positively or negatively impact the people you meet within a very short period of time.
- When clients and prospects are asking themselves, "How credible is the presenter?" the first thing they look at is your clothing.
- It is important to consider adapting your style of dress to the people you are addressing; dress in a style that is polished but similar to that of your listeners.

- Before you even think about fashion, you should focus on having an outfit that is well fitted.
- It's a great idea to dress up in order to show honor and respect for your clients' time.
- Clothing consultants can give you advice pertaining to color, style, and even protocol for dress requirements for varying presentations and situations.
- Dressing well may require a small financial investment at first but it is one that will pay you back many times over. When you look and feel great when you walk in the door for a presentation the boost to your energy and confidence will help you put the finishing touches on a great presentation.

Next: Wearing inappropriate dress is the last of our nine biggest mistakes that sales professionals make, and I hope you will take its importance to heart. The next chapter is devoted to the means for implementing some of the advice given earlier in the book. I have a system for doing a self-evaluation that managers can employ with their staff or individuals can use after recording their presentations on videotape.

How to Do a Self-Evaluation

Self-knowledge is the beginning of self-improvement.
—Spanish proverb

I n this chapter you will find a Presentation Evaluation Chart that will help you to analyze your own presentation skills, or those of your employees, to determine areas that may need improvement.

The best way to start an evaluation is to break out your home video camera and engage in a role-playing exercise, with a friend or associate serving as your audience. Of course I realize that the mere thought of being videotaped sends many people into panic, so before we get started with what criteria to employ in the evaluation, let's address a little problem for presenters—nervousness.

People say to me, "Terri, I get extremely nervous whenever I speak, not only before a live audience but also in front of a video camera. I understand how my presentation should be laid out, that I must incorporate stories, anecdotes, humor, and drama in order to bring the presentation to life, but when I start thinking about delivering it in front of a video camera, it really makes me nervous." Don't worry—this reaction is extremely common.

Effects of Nervousness

Among common fears, most people rank public speaking up there with falling out of an airplane. I have seen people become panicky to the point of paralysis during video training sessions. In one of our sessions, a woman literally started crying; in another, I was afraid the man was going to have a heart attack. Certain people are more anxious about giving talks than others. However, even the most callous politician gets a little nervous before making a presentation. There are two things to remember about nervousness: first, it is completely normal, and, second, a variation of it is likely to stay with you as long as you give presentations.

If you have ever competed in sports, you know that you always are going to be a little nervous before a game or a race no matter how good you become. The best people in any competitive activity are nervous before an event. Giving a good sales presentation is competitive so by its very nature it will cause some nervousness. The better prepared you are, however, the less nervous you will be.

Let's take a closer look at the symptoms of nervousness and their apparent causes. A dry throat is a sign, as are moist palms, fluttery stomach (even nausea), shortness of breath, and feet that feel like lead. Look in the mirror and see if your face is red. It is probably nerves.

Some People Are More Nervous

Some people get more nervous in front of a group than others do. We call these individuals *high communication-*

apprehension people. Others are more laid back, and we refer to them as *low communication-apprehension people.*

Each of us has a different personality and will react differently to the same situation. In extreme cases of high communication-apprehension, a person has to ask herself if sales is the right business to be in. Not everyone will get used to speaking in public, even one-on-one. That is why some people choose low-visibility positions.

The main thing is to try public speaking, implement the techniques in this book, and monitor whether your anxiety starts diminishing. Most people will adjust to the stress, but not everyone. The woman who broke down in tears during our training session probably will get over that extreme reaction, but she has a longer road ahead than someone for whom public speaking is effortless.

Keep It to Yourself

Divulging your apprehension before your presentation is not going to help you. Listeners don't know you are nervous if you don't let them in on the secret. You don't look nervous to them, and they won't know what you don't tell them. If you have to be open about it, tell them afterward. Telling listeners that you are nervous is not going to convince them. It may lead them to believe you are nervous because you are not competent. People believe that the opposite of being nervous is feeling confident and, therefore, capable.

Do's and Don'ts for Controlling Anxiety

Here are a few do's and don'ts to help you control your anxiety.

Do...

- Take your time.
- Move to refocus your concentration.

- Aim for variety in gesturing.
- Modulate your voice.
- Allow your body to talk.
- Have a sense of humor about yourself.
- Speak clearly; enunciate each word.

DON'T...

- Confess you are nervous.
- Apologize.
- Panic.
- Pace back and forth.
- Cross your arms.
- Fiddle with pens, pencils, papers.
- Rush.

Remember that when you are nervous, you are under stress. When you are under stress, you are learning new things. As the saying goes, "No pain, no gain." If you aren't nervous and don't feel uncomfortable, you aren't pushing your limits, and you aren't growing.

Seven Reasons for Being Nervous

There are various reasons why people feel nervous during a talk. We can point to a few obvious ones:

1. Lack of preparation.
2. A general lack of self-confidence.
3. Lack of self-confidence about a specific ability.
4. Fear of failing.
5. Fear of inadequacy.
6. Fear of embarrassment.
7. Fear of being evaluated poorly.

Yet even when all of these issues are put to rest as well as humanly possible, we still find that we are nervous. As we scratch a little deeper for a reason beneath the surface, we realize how terribly exposed and vulnerable we feel in front of a major client or group. We know it is up to us to carry the weight of the entire dialogue.

It is common knowledge that before competition we are filled with contradictory emotions: the fear of failure and the desire for success. There is little question that giving a presentation is exciting.

Professor's Lecture

When I was doing research at Cal State Long Beach while working on my master's degree, I had the opportunity to hear a visiting professor of Speech Communication. He talked about his research into fear and anxiety generated by public speaking. What he found was that whenever you speak or present your body may experience a massive adrenaline rush. Now, according to this professor's research, this release of adrenaline is so intense when you are giving a talk that it is matched by only one other occasion in your life—romantic intimacy. According to the research, during a major speech or presentation you can experience an adrenaline rush that is equal to that of what you produce at the height of sexual arousal. (So, if you're love life has been a little sideways, maybe you should go out and give more sales presentations!) The difference between the nervousness we feel before romance and what precedes a speech is just that we know how to channel the energy that develops before romance. We can also learn how to channel the energy that develops before giving a presentation.

Success Is What Matters

One important thing to reiterate is that it is not how nervous you are that counts, it is how successfully you deliver your presentation. Being open with the audience about your nervous feelings may hinder your success. The idea is to make your best effort for the best outcome, whether it is a signed contract, a follow-up appointment, or an audience prepared to go out and vote for your candidate.

Your audience determines whether you are successful, and to win their applause you will have to appear polished. When I say someone is polished, I mean he or she has a smooth flow and a strong command of the material, the audience, the environment, and the timing—overall, he or she has a presence that is commanding.

Becoming a Polished Speaker

I see people during training who give presentations that are incredibly sloppy. There are several reasons, and the first one is they simply don't care. They are going to coast, not really trying to look good or sound good. Unfortunately, it's obvious to the audience. In so many words, they are saying to their listeners, "I don't care if I waste your time."

In order to become a polished speaker you must *desire* to become one—you have to care about how you are perceived. You have to care about your audience, whether it is made up of one person or a hundred people.

The second reason people don't give strong presentations is they don't have a clear idea what they should be doing. Nor are they able to see what they actually are doing. They aren't aware of how bad they look or sound. They don't have a vision of how good they could be. This is why we are providing you with a Presentation Evaluation Chart, so that you can analyze and evaluate your current abilities and set new goals for the future.

The third reason people give poor presentations is that they just haven't committed to enough practice to be able to do it right. Knowledge, practice, and the will to improve—does that sound familiar? Of course it does; these are the same three qualities necessary to achieve anything worthwhile.

Let's face it. Giving a good presentation is challenging. If it were easy, everyone would be doing it. The opportunity for you as a sales professional, however, is to use this skill to increase your closing ratio (and your income) and to motivate others to act on your ideas. Those are powerful incentives for someone to accept such a challenge. And you will improve significantly if you implement the techniques in this book.

The subtle quality of a true power speaker is charisma—the mesmerizing charm a person expresses in the presence of another. Charisma comes from self-confidence—the certainty of knowing what is happening and what is about to happen. Self-confidence emerges with polish—control over thought, voice, and appearance. All these characteristics find their common root in individual practice.

Polish is also achieved through your professional/personal etiquette before, during, and after your presentations. For a good reference guide on the subject, read *Corporate Protocol: A Brief Case for Business Etiquette* by Valerie Grant-Sokolosky.

Following is a list of 21 points to consider in your quest to become a more polished and powerful speaker.

21 KEYS TO A MORE POWERFUL PRESENTATION STYLE

1. Believe in everything you say and represent.
2. Set objectives.
3. Plan the best approach.
4. Establish time limits.
5. Craft the introduction carefully.
6. Organize your presentation into a logical outline.
7. Use humor, anecdotes, and stories.
8. Select speech supports appropriate to the audience.
9. Clearly summarize information.
10. Encourage listener participation.
11. Ensure all facts and statistics are scrupulously accurate.
12. Express vitality with your voice.
13. Evaluate the attitudes and needs of your audience.
14. Provide enduring conclusions.
15. Vary your pace.

16. Speak clearly and distinctly.
17. Be lively and enthusiastic.
18. Be clear when moving from point to point.
19. Don't oversell; use a conversational approach.
20. Use variation in your vocabulary.
21. Find a public speaking role model.

Using a Presentation Evaluation Chart

The evaluation chart on the following pages can be used alone employing a video camera to tape your talk or by having a friend evaluate how well you do. Try using it to evaluate other speakers' presentations. This will help you become increasingly sensitive to the various elements of a good sales presentation. Do a simple self-evaluation of your next presentation. Do you commit any of the listed mistakes while speaking to your clients or prospects? When you can identify the weaknesses in your presentation, you can begin to correct them. As a result, you will become more confident, polished, and persuasive, and more consistent in delivering effective presentations.

If you are an individual interested in improving your presentation style, give your presentation in front of a video camera. If you don't own a camcorder, find someone who has one and ask if you can borrow it. Then watch your presentation. At the end, critically review your performance as you would any speaker using the Presentation Evaluation Chart.

If you are a manager and you want to use the chart to improve the performance of your team, have each person give his or her presentation either in your presence, in front of another team member, or before the entire group. Let the audience use the chart to evaluate the performance. If this scenario is too blunt for some of the more sensitive members of the group, have them give their presentations on video, then hand them the chart to evaluate their own performance.

NINE BIGGEST MISTAKES PRESENTATION EVALUATION CHART

CONTENT	Excellent	Good	Average	Poor
Mistake No. 1—Winging It				
Could you follow the main theme throughout the entire presentation?	❏	❏	❏	❏
Did the speaker cover all relevant points?	❏	❏	❏	❏
Did the presentation have a logical progressive flow?	❏	❏	❏	❏
Mistake No. 2—Being Too Informative versus Persuasive				
Was there good interaction with the audience?	❏	❏	❏	❏
Did the speaker build a persuasive case and implement harms?	❏	❏	❏	❏
Was the presentation convincing?	❏	❏	❏	❏
Mistake No. 4—Providing Inadequate Support				
Did you note the use of speech supports such as anecdotes, analogies, and testimonials?	❏	❏	❏	❏
Did the speaker use convincing evidence?	❏	❏	❏	❏
Did the audience believe the speaker was credible, and could they relate to him/her?	❏	❏	❏	❏
Mistake No. 5—Failing to Close the Sale				
Did the presentation have both a conclusion and a close?	❏	❏	❏	❏
Was the presentation designed to be persuasive throughout?	❏	❏	❏	❏

(Continued)

NINE BIGGEST MISTAKES PRESENTATION EVALUATION CHART *(Continued)*

Were the listeners asked to take
action at the end of the
presentation? ❑ ❑ ❑ ❑

PERFORMANCE	Excellent	Good	Average	Poor

Mistake No. 3—Misusing the Allotted Time

	Excellent	Good	Average	Poor
Did the introduction grab your attention?	❑	❑	❑	❑
Did the speaker stay within the prescribed time limits?	❑	❑	❑	❑
Were there at least three distinct body points separated by transitions?	❑	❑	❑	❑

Mistake No. 6—Being Boring, Boring, Boring

	Excellent	Good	Average	Poor
Did the speaker tailor the presentation to meet the needs of the audience?	❑	❑	❑	❑
Did the speaker have good diction and control over tone and volume?	❑	❑	❑	❑
Was there energy and enthusiasm in the presenter's delivery?	❑	❑	❑	❑
Was there an emotional conclusion to the presentation?	❑	❑	❑	❑
Were you ever bored?	No	❑	Yes	❑

Mistake No. 7—Relying Too Much on Visual Aids

	Excellent	Good	Average	Poor
Did the speaker maintain control of the presentation when using visual aids?	❑	❑	❑	❑

NINE BIGGEST MISTAKES PRESENTATION EVALUATION CHART *(Continued)*

Was the number of aids used appropriate to enhance the message?	❏	❏	❏	❏
Did the presenter have control over the technical aspects of a computer presentation?	❏	❏	❏	❏
How relevant were the visual aids?	❏	❏	❏	❏

Mistake No. 8—Distracting Gestures and Body Language

Did the speaker keep control of hands and avoid distracting body movements?	❏	❏	❏	❏
Did the speaker maintain strong eye contact with audience members?	❏	❏	❏	❏
Did the speaker move with purpose before the audience?	❏	❏	❏	❏

Mistake No. 9—Wearing Inappropriate Dress

Were the presenter's clothes clean and pressed and shoes shined?	❏	❏	❏	❏
Was presenter's attire appropriate to the industry, audience, and event?	❏	❏	❏	❏
Were the colors of the presenter's clothing coordinated, tasteful, and appealing?	❏	❏	❏	❏

COMMENTS

How was the overall presentation?

_____

_____

_____

Overview

- Performing a self-evaluation of your presentations will help you identify the strengths and weaknesses in both your content and delivery style.
- Feelings of nervousness are normal. Just remember that with practice and preparation, you can lessen the amount of nervousness you will experience.
- Review the 21 keys to a more powerful presentation to help you stay focused on your presentation goals.
- The Presentation Evaluation Chart included in this chapter has been designed to help you to identify and avoid the nine biggest sales presentation mistakes. It can also help you create a more consistent pattern of successful presentations.
- Have fun, enjoy the learning experiences, and re-member—you can do it!

Next: With the Nine Biggest Mistakes Presentation Evaluation Chart and the criteria necessary to judge the effectiveness of any presentation, you should have the means to improve your ability to persuade people to buy your products, services, or ideas. Let's turn now to the final chapter to sum up and review what you have learned.

Final Thoughts

No pessimist ever discovered the secrets of the stars, or sailed to an uncharted land or opened a new heaven to the human spirit.

—Helen Keller

The story I recounted in Chapter 1 about gaining access to a residential real estate organization by presenting the president with a white rose is more than just an anecdote on the importance of novel ways of approaching people. It is about making people feel special. When you are original, sincere, and credible, you bestow on people the caring respect they deserve as individuals.

Greg Dell Story

A client and friend named Greg Dell sells high-ticket computer software that provides solutions for large corporate printing needs. The sales cycle typically is lengthy, and he has to make presentations to different levels of management within the organization. Greg is well familiar with the nine biggest mistakes presenters make and has developed his persuasive skills to be very effective within the challenging corporate environment. Sometimes, however, he has found that even though he has followed all the rules, covered all the bases, and given presentations to all the right decision-makers, he still can't seem to get the client to make a decision. This is sometimes in spite of the fact it would frequently save the client thousands of dollars every month.

On one such occasion Greg finally decided that what was needed was not more information, but more energy to move the sale on to the next step. Greg knew the computing department managers he was talking to wanted his product, but they were going to have to get it approved by higher-ups. Taking a line from the Tom Cruise movie *Jerry Maguire*, in which Cruise plays a high-powered professional sports agent, Greg began to act out the scene in front of his clients in which Jerry pleads with his hard-to-manage athlete, "Help me, help you. Help *me*, help you!" With Greg waving his arms in the normally staid computing environment, everyone in the room cracked up laughing, and in no time they were able to secure the necessary approvals. The stunt worked because Greg was willing to go over the top and infuse the situation with so much energy that his clients felt obliged to match his effort aimed at completing the sale. After working with Greg all the way up to this point, they simply had to *do something* in order to help him complete the transaction. While you may think this behavior is a bit exaggerated, it was appropriate because of the long-term selling cycle and the rapport Greg had built with the prospects . . . his energy was so infectious they wanted to work with him and his company. Remember that people buy people.

Pearls of Wisdom

Following are several interviews with people who have mastered the art of persuasive presentations. Each has honed the skills important to giving a truly dazzling presentation, and all have become experts in the field of sales. In these pearls of wisdom they have shared with me (for the express purpose of sharing with you) how these skills, traits, and behaviors we have been discussing can be put to use in a variety of different sales environments. They show how our keys to success can have a significant effect on selling your product, service, idea, or philosophy—or yourself—to a prospective client, customer, or employer.

Jerry Anderson

The first interview is with Jerry Anderson, president of Coldwell Banker Commercial real estate brokerage company. Jerry was kind enough to share with me his experience using advanced sales techniques. His story of how he came to be in charge of a $300 million real estate company is a textbook example of how individuals using persuasive communication skills can rise to the top of their field, thus benefiting not only themselves but thousands of others whose futures benefit from the success of their ideas.

TERRI SJODIN: Jerry, we've had the opportunity to speak in the past about the amazing transformation of Coldwell Banker Commercial and your role in that transformation. I was hoping you could give us a brief overview of the story, so that we can learn through your experience of how your ability to sell your ideas helped you make a big career transition and affected the success of a large organization.

JERRY ANDERSON: I think the story of Coldwell Banker Commercial really illustrates how important it is to sell an idea, a philosophy, and then implement that philosophy. Here is a little background. About 1990, Coldwell Banker Real Estate Corp. sold its commercial division to a group of managers. This left the corporation in only the residential real estate field. Because they sold off the commercial arm of the business, they were now contractually prohibited for a period of time from reentering the commercial business. The business that was sold was renamed CB Richard Ellis, which today is a formidable competitor in the field of commercial real estate.

After the non-compete clause expired, however, Coldwell Banker Real Estate Corp. began entertaining thoughts of reentering the commercial market, but in a different way. The parent company, Cendant, is a franchiser. It owns a number of brands, including eight hotel brands and three residential real estate brands. Now they wanted to structure a commercial real estate company under the same successful structure.

So where do I come in? I had worked as a middle manager in the corporate real estate environment, but I left because I was frustrated that the company would not implement many of my ideas, which I felt were extremely good ones. I decided I would become a consultant and sell my ideas to other firms in the field. I did that for about eight years, was on retainer with two or three major commercial real estate companies, and was earning a good income. The beauty of being a consultant is that you give your client your best strategies and ideas, you hope they implement them, but if they don't, they still continue to pay you as long as you keep giving them ideas.

The best part of being a consultant is that you have the opportunity to see the very best ideas being discussed by all the companies in the field. As a consultant, you can, in effect, repackage those ideas and sell them. Not only are you better informed because you know what the industry is doing, but also you can then deliver more knowledge to your clients.

When Coldwell Banker Real Estate Corp. wanted to get back into the commercial business, I was hired as a consultant to give them advice. So I told them what I thought should be done. Some of the advice they took— but some of the advice they didn't pay much attention to. Nevertheless, by 1997, they had a national group of commercial real estate companies operating as franchises generating forty million dollars a year in gross commissions. As a consultant, however, I was frustrated because I saw the operation as having a potential to do much better.

The name Coldwell Banker Commercial had been around since the early 1900s. It is a company that is almost one hundred years old with a legacy of excellence. I felt the parent company was not really taking advantage of that track record. Though they would implement some of my ideas, what disturbed me the most was the philosophy of the parent company. The rekindled commercial company was completely different from what it had been in the past. Historically, the company would dominate its market share. It was always working in the client's best interest, and it would really provide a high level of service to its clientele. I recognized that philosophy was missing.

One day, out of frustration, I went to the CEO of Coldwell Banker Real Estate Corp, and said, "I have an idea, and it's one that I believe will take this unpolished gem of a company you own, a gem now lying in the dirt doing only forty million dollars a year in gross revenues, and polish it up so that the commercial real estate company will not only regroup to where it was in prior years but will be in a position to grow and take advantage of change for the next several years."

TS: Was he receptive to hearing your ideas initially?

ANDERSON: He was receptive because I was a consultant. But, they had never viewed me as anything more than a consultant. So, I put together a PowerPoint presentation that was very logical that basically went something like this:

"There are three reasons why Coldwell Banker Commercial needs to be the number-one commercial real estate company in the world. The first reason is that we have almost a century of legacy just lying here that we are not taking advantage of. [They needed to revitalize the branding of Coldwell Banker Commercial.]

"The number-two reason is that Coldwell Banker Commercial is owned by one of the world's largest enterprises of consumer interest, the Cendant Corporation, which is a twenty-billion-dollar company. We're not taking full advantage of this ownership. [The strength, the backing, the credibility, the financial assets, and the synergies of the parent company's other brands were not being strategically used to full advantage.]

"The third reason is that I believe there are many people in local markets who know the name, and if we provide those clients with a strong office in their locale, they will once again gravitate back to Coldwell Banker Commercial and therefore make the organization more profitable. [To create strong local offices, we had to reattract the best sales agents by providing superior branding, credibility, and support services.]"

I presented my case to corporate, and I also presented the philosophy that the company had operated under for almost a century—nothing new, just a reaffirmation of what had made it great in the past.

They bought into that philosophy, but there was a third part to my presentation. After eight years of consulting, I felt the need to finally get in and make some things happen. One frustration I had as a consultant was that I would give great advice, people would pay me for it, but they would not implement it. As a consultant, I wasn't on the payroll. I didn't have the authority or the control. I couldn't delegate or implement: I could just tell people what they *should* do. It was the typical responsibility-without-authority dilemma.

So, the third part of my presentation beyond presenting the ideas and philosophy was that I wanted to be the implementer. I wanted to be the CEO of this new company. I wanted to be the president of Coldwell Banker Commercial so that I could implement. I wanted to be, if you will, the captain of the ship. I knew what all the competitors were doing. They were taking my advice. They were taking their respective ideas and making them better. I could take all of the ideas and the best traits of all our competitors and bring them to Coldwell Banker Commercial.

TS: So, really you were selling yourself and you were selling a philosophy and you were selling an idea.

ANDERSON: Right. Next, I had to sell them on the required investment. Here was a company that hadn't invested much in the Coldwell Banker Commercial brand, and here I am a young whippersnapper saying, "Okay, number one, you need to do this, and number two, you need to do that, and number three, you need to hire me to implement it. And by the way, I need an additional group of support people, and it is going to cost you $1 million to get that team underway. And, by the way, we need that check by the end of the month." It was not an easy sell.

However, once I showed them that we really had an unpolished gem, that Cendant could back us financially, and showed them the opportunity that was available, it was possible for them to say, "Jerry, you come to work for us, you take charge, you hire the additional staff you need. Bring in the new companies that you want, you reinstill the philosophy that the company used to have—and we will back you financially." And they did.

The results speak for themselves. In 1997, Coldwell Banker Commercial's gross commission revenue was forty million dollars. In 1998, under my leadership, the gross commissions went up to eighty-two million. In 1999, our gross commissions rose to one-hundred-eighty-five million dollars. In the year 2000, we did approximately three-hundred-ten million—all this within about thirty-six months after my initial presentation.

TS: Did they question you or give you a hard time about why you should be the one to do it? Were you ever concerned that they would buy the idea but they wouldn't buy you?

ANDERSON: Well you always have concerns about that. It was a question of which comes first, the chicken or the egg. Once I presented my great strategy, would they have confidence in me to implement it? I could only find out one way. I believe I had a step up, however, because I was a trusted consultant. The other thing that helped me was having been highly regarded as a trainer.

I had done some training at their conferences and the survey feedback from the audience ranked me as the number-one presenter. I also believe my strong ability to present my ideas in a training classroom carried into the boardroom as I was selling my implementation and philosophy.

TS: You said there were three ideas you used in building your initial presentation. Did you also specify what the harms were—what terrible, horrible things would happen if they didn't implement your ideas?

ANDERSON: While building the three main reasons why they should do this, I constantly would flip to the negative side and say, "You know, here is a century's worth of legacy, and every day that we let this gem lie in the dirt, it gets dirtier and dirtier and dirtier. In people's minds, the further away we get from what the company used to be, the less valuable it will be to us in the future."

The other thing I did was explain how the commercial real estate industry is finite in size, and that there are only so many agents. It's very difficult to recruit. I told them that if we didn't build this company, those agents would go to our competitors. So, again, part of selling the three reasons why they should do this was that if we built strong local companies in local markets, people/clients would flock back to us. Obviously, part of this was in attracting the agents. So, the harms that I created were really based on one idea—that "every day that goes by, we lose the opportunity to build a strong company from what we used to be. And people's memories are short." I also pointed out that there are a finite number of agents, and if we didn't put this company in place, those agents would wind up somewhere else.

TS: In other words, the company could lose value by waiting. You could lose the people, and in fact, that would mean losing money and market share.

ANDERSON: Correct.

TS: Did they think they had a problem before you presented it, or were they thinking that everything was fine?

ANDERSON: The leadership knew that they had a problem because they realized that it was not the company that it could be. By no means did they realize we could have the skyrocket growth that we have had. In fact, our chairman of the board likes to point out the fact that Coldwell Banker Commercial is one of the brands that was, figuratively speaking, started in the back of a garage without a huge investment. You have to understand that enterprises that own multiple companies are used to paying hundreds of millions of dollars for a brand. We have a very strong brand without that type of an investment. We are much larger than they thought we would be, and it happened a lot faster than anybody ever imagined.

TS: Were you scared when you pitched this that you couldn't pull it off?

ANDERSON: I was scared because it made me nervous that I was the only one who saw this opportunity. I was nervous about finding out whether "either I was so smart that nobody else had seen it, or, I was so stupid that everybody else had already looked and figured out it can't happen."

TS: That is a wonderful revelation because I think a lot of people doubt their ideas. They think, "Wow, I have this idea—I can't believe nobody else sees it. Am I nuts for thinking I can do this?" It is a little intimidating because you are definitely breaking into uncharted territory.

ANDERSON: They were definitely uncharted waters. I can remember flying back after the interview thinking, "I am either the smartest guy in the industry or I am about to take a tumble." There was a risk because I was fairly comfortable and successful with my consulting efforts generating a half million dollars a year in fees.

TS: So, after you gave your presentation, did you close at the end by asking them to make a decision?

ANDERSON: Oh, yes, I am a salesperson. So, I asked for the order, in fact, I can remember the closing slide. I had a pair of shaking hands with the question, "When can we get started?" (I used the word "we"—when can *we* get started.) The implication was, "I am now joining 'the team' of Coldwell Banker Commercial—I want to implement." I basically used the closing question of timing.

TS: When you finished your presentation, did you have to go through an extensive question-and-answer session?

ANDERSON: There wasn't much of a Q&A—other than about the money. The main questions were:

Do you really need that much money?

Why can't we just limp along for a while?

Why do we have to hire such high-powered servicing people?

Why do we have to create this "group" to call on corporations?

Is it really necessary to do all of that to be successful?

TS: When you walked out the door, did they say, "Okay, we want to think about it, want to talk about it, and we'll get back to you"?

ANDERSON: The "think about it, talk about it, and get back to you" part was really in reference to the package that I wanted. Because I was leaving an environment of success, the one thing that did make me nervous was that I had built up a very strong consulting business over the last eight years, and I was about to walk away from it.

TS: How long did the whole process take?

ANDERSON: We moved forward in less than two weeks. The final interview was in the middle of April and by May 1, 1998, it was done.

TS: What do you think were the key factors in putting this together for you?

ANDERSON: The critical factor for me in this was the analogy of the unpolished gem. When I used the phrase "unpolished gem," two people who were sitting at the table started leaning forward and said, "We never thought of it like that before!"

I believe that if I had used the phrase "underutilized asset," nobody would have leaned forward. But when I said, "you own an unpolished gem lying in the dirt being kicked around that, if we were to pick it up, caress it, polish it and shape it—it could be extremely valuable." They all related to that analogy.

TS: Jerry, when you used to do consulting and speaking, I heard you say that selling is presenting, and presenting is selling—the two are tied together. We can't sell without a great presentation, and we can't present without having the right selling concepts to build our case on and to move forward. Does that still characterize what you do every day?

ANDERSON: It is exactly what I do everyday. I just got back from France where we opened an office in Paris, and we are now franchising in 11 different countries in Europe. We now have three offices in Israel. Trust me, when you leave your own soil to go to another country, you had better be able to present because you're now on their territory, and you had better be able to sell your ideas and your philosophies. So I am in the selling business every time I meet with a prospective franchisee because I'm selling our concept and our philosophy. I'm in the selling business, and it is through strong presentation skills that I am able to do that.

TS: I think it is ironic because most people would think, gee, you are the president of Coldwell Banker Commercial, and you still say that you are in sales. Most people would say, "I'm in management."

ANDERSON: I have to sell to my staff, to our franchise offices that we service, and to our associates on the fact that we constantly bring value. We are three thousand people strong in our organization. I believe that I am selling every single day to all three thousand of them.

TS: Are there some pearls of wisdom that you would like to impart to the readers?

ANDERSON: I think the pearl of wisdom is in the thought that, "I am either the smartest person in the industry or the most ignorant." That's where the pearl lies.

TS: In other words, if you have an idea, put it down on paper, build a solid case, present it with all of your heart and soul—in short, make it happen.

ANDERSON: That's it. Make something happen.

Brian Tracy

Our next interview is with Brian Tracy, one of today's most popular and respected speakers and sales trainers. Brian's audiotape program on sales training, The Psychology of Selling: The Art of Closing the Sale, *is among the most widely distributed in history. He has written numerous books, including the ever-popular* Maximum Achievement: Strategies and Skills That Will Unlock Your Hidden Powers to Succeed, *(Fireside, 1995). Among his latest hits to be published is* The 100 Absolutely Unbreakable Laws of Business Success. *One of my first sales jobs was promoting sales training seminars for Brian while working for The Achievement Group. In this interview, Brian shares his views on sales strategies and addresses special concerns in making a presentation to venture capitalists—an increasingly common challenge in today's growing dot-com economy.*

TERRI SJODIN: Thank you, Brian, for taking the time this morning to share your story with us.

BRIAN TRACY: Well, it's a pleasure to be talking with you. As you know, my sales career began as a young man when I couldn't get any other kind of job. I got no sales training, and I struggled for many months until I began asking, "Why is it that some salespeople are more successful than others?" Then I began asking other salespeople what they were doing differently from me—and they told me. So, instead of talking, I began asking questions. Instead of arguing, I began dealing with concerns in a more professional way. Then I began reading everything I could find—hundreds of books on selling. I began listening to all the audio programs that had been done and attending every sales course. What I found is that selling is a profession. It's a science with a methodology and a practice, and if you do what other successful salespeople do, you get the same results that other successful salespeople get. If you don't, you won't.

I then dedicated basically my entire career to finding out these cause-and-effect relationships. What enables some people to be more successful than others? My sales went up and up and up. I became a sales manager. I built a six-country sales force. In every case whenever I was stuck, I went and asked people or searched in books, "Why are some people more successful than others?"

What I found is that selling is a very simple process. It has a methodology and a process and if you follow it, you make more sales. In the last twenty-five years, millions and millions of dollars have been spent, including an enormous amount of money on my part, on interviewing customers to find out why it is they buy and why it is they don't buy. More than fifty-five thousand customers have been interviewed before and after sales presentations and asked, "What do you think will happen? What is your expectation?" Afterwards, if they bought, they were asked: "Why did they buy?" If they didn't buy they were asked, "Why didn't they buy?"

What we find is that if you can take a person who has never sold anything before and simply give them a methodology and a process to follow, then they will become successful salespeople. The critical thing is that they be able to discipline themselves to follow a process—a process of separating prospects from suspects, so to speak. A process involves asking questions to find out if the prospect is genuinely interested in or can benefit from what you're selling. It then involves asking another series of questions to find out exactly "what they are using today to handle their problem, how it is working, what they intend to do, and what they are most concerned with." The process then involves showing them that your product or service is the ideal solution for what they want to accomplish. It's not a miracle; it's simply a process.

The problem with most salespeople is they get carried away and they talk and talk and talk. Surprise! The customer begins to lose interest. The fastest way to create a lack of interest in a customer is to start talking about things that the customer is not interested in.

TS: You make a great point. One of the things we found in our research was that among the leading reasons why someone didn't want to work with a particular salesperson was that their presentation was boring. The listener just tuned the salesperson out. It went too long. It was monotonous. It didn't meet their specific needs. It was, bottom line, boring.

TRACY: You find that if you ask really good questions, and listen carefully to the answers, eventually customers will tell you everything you need to know either to make the sale or determine that this is not an appropriate person to sell to. I often use what I call the "doctor of selling approach." As a doctor, first you do an examination, then you do a diagnosis, with which the client should agree. Then you present a possible solution. It follows that order: examination, diagnosis, and prescription. Many salespeople, however, go straight from "hello" to "prescription."

TS: Now, one of the questions that may come up is, "Brian, you have had such a super-successful sales organization, but do you still consider yourself a sales professional?"

TRACY: Well, I sell all the time. First of all, I sell my services as a professional speaker and as a consultant and trainer, and I also sell my services and my programs from the front of the room to hundreds of people. Yesterday, I did a sales presentation for four hundred people. Usually in a matter of twelve or fifteen minutes I will sell between ten thousand and twenty thousand dollars' worth of program materials. I use a specific methodology and process to do that type of a presentation for people who up to that minute have never thought about buying a program and then, fifteen minutes later, will spend several thousand dollars on program materials. There is a methodology, which is to start off by pointing out that they can be "vastly more effective in what they are doing through the help of these programs." Then you show them the program and show what is in it. Then you explain how they can benefit from it and give examples of people who have benefited from it. Then you ask them to make a buy decision.

TS: One of the things you talk about is that it is a series of little wins that together add up to a big win. Has there ever been a situation where there was a big win for you? In your career, over thirty years as a speaker, you've had an amazing consistency in winning, but have there ever been any big wins that really stood out, that you thought of as a really pivotal time?

TRACY: I find that there are no great breakthroughs or explosions where the earth moves and the clouds part and you have a big deal. My success has been really a matter of doing hundreds and thousands of little things over and over again, year after year. There has never been a great breakthrough. Perhaps a turning point was when Nightingale Conant first offered to sell one of my programs. That was helpful, but the reason that happened was because of a whole series of meetings with them, telephone calls, going there and visiting with them, talking to people, and then their finally deciding, tentatively, to try out the program. The reason why the relationship has been successful is because the programs sold well. But there is no one big lightning strike.

I've had many people ask me over the years, "Brian, when does the explosion take place? When does the big moment take place?" These people have been reading too many comic books. The fact is that in your career and in my career there is no one big moment. If you try a hundred things, every so often you will try something that is much more successful than average, and then you go back to work again. As my friend Dennis says, "Success is never permanent, and failure is never final." It's an ongoing process and every successful person I know just works at it all day long, every day, year after year—no great breakthroughs.

I just hired a sales professional who has absolutely no fear of rejection. He has developed a step-by-step process to establish a relationship and rapport to identify what it is that the customer needs, to make recommendations, and to encourage the customer to give it a try. No matter how many times people tell him that they're not interested, or they want to think it over, it doesn't bother him at all. He is absolutely unstoppable. And this is very, very important.

TS: You mean being tenacious?

TRACY: Yes, having tenacity. The larger the product the more background work, planning, preparation is necessary. The smaller the product, the greater frequency of contact is necessary to uncover the right prospects. Therefore if you're selling a big product where one sale can make an enormous amount of difference, then you do a lot of preparation. If you are selling a little product, then you increase your rate of activity and you see and talk to as many people as possible.

TS: When you're interviewing people, do you look for qualities of how well they sell themselves as a criterion of whether you should hire them?

TRACY: Yes. I think the most important qualities for successful salespeople are optimism and persistence, which really go hand in hand. A person with a really good attitude who is persistent, is not afraid to try and keep trying, is a person who is going to be far more successful and is someone who can be trained in anything. The rule is, "You always hire for attitude and personality, and everything else can be learned."

TS: So, what do you say to the idea that would have us believe that "salespeople are born, not made?"

TRACY: Well, Peter Drucker once said, "There is such a thing as a born leader, but there are so few of them, that they make no difference in the great scheme of things." I think for salespeople it's the same. I've seen people who have gone from being accountants, or electricians, or plumbers, or carpenters, or even car repairmen to becoming superb salespeople.

TS: Has there ever been a salesperson who sort of leaped out at you making you think, "By gosh, that guy had a great approach," or "He was really creative"? Have you ever had the experience where a salesperson really dazzled you?

TRACY: Not really. I think the very best salespeople are very professional. They're very knowledgeable. They're very warm and friendly. They exude a tremendous sense of self-confidence because they really know their business. They've taken the time to do their homework, and because they are so confident in themselves they cause the customer to feel a great sense of confidence in whatever they are selling. Good salespeople in many cases sell even before they open their mouth. People think, "Whatever that person is offering, I feel comfortable with it already."

In America, there are two great fears that all customers have that every salesperson must overcome initially. First is the fear of being taken advantage of. The reason people have this fear is because they have been taken advantage of so many times. They have bought the wrong product. They have paid the wrong price. They have gotten poor follow-up service. They have found it cheaper somewhere else. They have found a product that did a better job somewhere else. So, every single customer today has made a thousand buying mistakes in his or her past, starting from childhood. They've regretted them and they've made the decision: "That's not going to happen again." Then you walk in, and all of their previous buying mistakes are suddenly refreshed. They remember them when they look at you and talk to you, so they're very, very nervous about being taken advantage of. The second great fear that customers have is being hustled, being manipulated or being talked into doing something that is not of great advantage to them.

So, you have those two fears going in. When you meet a customer for the first time, that's why there is the initial resistance, even in a customer who is interested in the product. So, the very best salespeople are those who structure their approach and their personality in such a way that the customer relaxes and does not fear being either manipulated or taken advantage of.

TS: What is a common mistake that you feel salespeople make?

TRACY: Well, I think the biggest mistake salespeople make in every single survey, in every study, is that they start talking about the product or service that they are selling before they are absolutely clear about what it is that the customer needs and wants. They go from examination to prescription without doing a proper diagnosis.

TS: Do you feel that the selling that you did in the past has brought you to the place where you are now?

TRACY: Oh, yes. When you begin, you have to be very organized, from the planning of your prospecting sales call on the telephone right through to the development of the presentation to the resolving of concerns and asking for the order and the delivery. You have to do a hundred percent of that. I used to have to do that two decades ago. But, over time you get to the point where you start further down in the process. Now, thanks to the excellent support I have, when my prospects come to me they are already done with stages three, four, and five. They've already qualified. They already know what they want and are going through a selection process.

TS: One of the people we talked with is getting ready to launch an initial public offering [IPO]. That requires his going back and building a great presentation because Wall Street is unforgiving, and you have a very short period of time to dazzle them with your road show. It is why you must know how to sell yourself, your company, and your organization. Do you have any comments on this specific type of requirement that is becoming more common in today's dot-com economy?

TRACY: When you talk about presentation skills and IPOs, today people are very busy and they have basically four questions: First, What is it? (They want to know what the product or service you're selling is.) Second, What's in it for me? Third, Who else has done it? Fourth, What do I get? And then the follow-on questions after that are: How fast, and how sure? A good presentation, whether or not for an IPO (and I'm involved in a couple), is very clear about those things. You should be able to do an ideal presentation, as they say, "in an elevator ride." You should be able to get right to the point. What most people do is spend an enormous amount of time talking about what they are going to talk about instead of getting right to the point.

An IPO presentation has special characteristics. Certain investment companies will book presentations every twelve minutes. They will have people lined up outside almost like central casting, who come in and have literally twelve minutes to make a presentation to an IPO committee or to a venture capital committee. This is a very different form of presenting from the type of selling we've been talking about. But all selling really begins with establishing rapport with the client, identifying the client's problem or need by asking questions and listening, and finding out what the client wants to accomplish. Of course that future state is inconsistent with where they are now—this is called the *gap analysis*. Then you have to show them that your product or service is the ideal solution for their problem. The order in which you do that has to follow that sequence. I say it's very much like a combination lock. If you have the right numbers, but you turn to them in the wrong order, the lock won't open. Therefore, salespeople have to be disciplined to follow in that order. For a really big sale they will spend the first two meetings simply establishing rapport. Only at the third meeting will they start talking about how these companies can work together. How can one company help the other? Sometimes they will even go to presenting and talking about how their products and services fit into the company's needs. Always the process is the same. Millions of dollars have been spent showing that if you try to sell outside the process of buying, if you try to sell in a way that is inconsistent with customers' way of buying, they won't buy anything.

The most important thing in an IPO, for example, if you're speaking to venture capitalists, their questions are, "How are you going to generate revenue with your idea? If I give you money, how am I going to get my money back?"

So, the very first thing you have to show is that your product or service is unique and special in such a way that a lot of people are going to buy it at very high margins and that you are going to make a great profit from it. It's very clear. For instance, you say we are going to offer prescription drugs on the Web so that people can buy prescription drugs of the same quality they can get at their pharmacy but at forty to fifty percent off. And you say that we are going to market this through every doctor and HMO in the country so that we will have forty to fifty million potential buyers of prescription drugs using our services, and that our profit margins will be this, this, and this. Then a person can make a decision—"That sounds like a great idea."

Or, someone comes up with something else, say they are going to sell toys. The profit model has to be very clear—every business has a profit model. This is the way that we are going to make profits. The profits are how you, as an investor, are going to be rewarded for your risk.

The second issue is, who is going to fulfill it? Who is the management? Who are the people who are going to deliver the goods? You have to show these are the people who are going to make this work and show their experience, background, and knowledge because that's the "how sure" part of the question. In short, it's first, how much?—that's the profit model—then, how sure? Well, if you have really top people, those people will make it work. If you have people with great success records in the past, these people will make it work, even if they have to change it to do so.

The third thing you show them is, "how fast?" How quickly are you going to get your money back? A good IPO presentation is, "Here's the business model, here are the people, and here is how the money is going to come back."

TS: What would you say is the average length of time for a good IPO presentation?

TRACY: There is no answer to that. It's like saying, what's the average length of time for a date? No one knows.

TS: One of the things people ask is, "How much time?" It depends on a couple of different things, one being how much time they will give you.

TRACY: Exactly. Whether they give you twelve minutes will depend on what you do with the first two minutes. Whether they give you two hours will depend on what you do with the twelve minutes. So, most venture capitalists will have committees to interview people all day long. Of the ten thousand business plans submitted to venture capitalists for funding, twelve will be picked. They will not even meet with the others and very often it's because their presentations are unclear. I have a business plan here from one company that is sixty pages long. It's ninety-eight percent gobbledygook. You almost need to be a detective to wade through and to find out exactly what the business is and how the money is going to come back. A really good presentation can be summarized on the back of a business card.

TS: I have heard that they want to see a great plan with a great strategy, but they are also looking for a great deal of passion. Do you believe that to be true?

TRACY: They are looking for a leader, a person who is going to make this happen. A person with a tremendous passion for what they are going to do with an Internet site is far more effective in convincing people than a techie who tries to explain some of the technical specifications of how it will work. Because everything ultimately, Terri, comes down to selling. I have had this argument over and over again and I say: In the final analysis, you have to sell something to someone and collect money to make a profit. You must keep focused on that like a laser beam. Everything has to be focused on selling something. So, it has to be easy to sell and easy to buy. It has to offer the purchaser definite improvements. It has to be faster, it has to be cheaper, it has to be easier, and it has to be more efficient.

In order to sell a new product against an existing product it has to be better by a factor of three. This is a very interesting concept. It says, basically, that before I buy product A, if I've been using product B, product A has to be better in three ways. So, what are the three factors that make product A superior to product B?

Many people think, "The reason to buy from me is because the product is super, or the reason to buy from me is because I want you to." But, you have to have three distinct reasons—one usually is not enough. It's almost like a triangle. So, when you ask salespeople what the three reasons why their product is superior to what their customers already are using, ninety-five percent of them have no idea. They pull something out of the air—*quality*. Well, quality is not a reason for buying anything. They might say, *service*. Well, service isn't a reason either. So, now why should somebody buy your product or service? Most salespeople have no idea. The problem is that all products offer quality and service so saying that yours has it is the same thing as saying "it comes in a box." So does everyone's. It's not a reason for buying it.

It used to be that you had to have very high quality to grow in the market. Today you have to have very high quality and service just to get into the market in the first place—just to exist. Those two are a given nowadays. So why should I buy? Because it's faster. Okay, that is important because there is a need for speed. Everybody is concerned about speed. This will achieve the result that you want to achieve faster than anything else that you're using. Okay, now you've got my attention. Not only is the product easier to use than anything else you have, but *ah-ha*! It's cheaper than anything else you can get. Now what you have is faster, cheaper, easier—the reason for success in all high-tech products, and the reason for success in all Internet startups. And the reason for failure is an absence of those three. If it's not easier, it's harder and more difficult. If it's not cheaper, it's actually more expensive. If it's not faster, it takes more time because it's so hard to figure out. So, every single company that is failing has failed on one of those three points.

TS: So, would you say that if someone were making a presentation to venture capitalists, where they were going to be pitching an Internet company, they should meet those three criteria?

TRACY: Sure. What you would say is, "Here's the market—demonstrated, proven, established by third-party independent figures. For example, the market in personal development products such as we sell is about four-point-two billion dollars, according to one of the recent surveys out of New York. We have a way to tap into this market with a product-service combination that is faster, cheaper, and easier than anything being offered today. So, we figure that within two years we can get five hundred million to one billion dollars' worth of that market with a profit ratio (profit margin or markup margin) of fifty percent. We reckon we can make two-fifty to five hundred million dollars a year within two years with our model." Now, that's the presentation. With that information, your client will say, "Hold my calls—tell me how you're going do it."

Most people don't realize what it takes. For example, I was given a fifty-page presentation that tries to say that and never gets to it. Consequently, nobody's even interested in a second meeting because they're not going to read the fifty pages. If you are not so crystal clear about how and why your product or service is faster, cheaper, and easier to use for a huge market that already exists—not a new market—but a huge market that already exists, and you're not so crystal clear you can't make that point to a skeptical, if not cynical investment banker on an elevator ride from the eighth floor to the ground, then you don't even know why you're out there. Most people in the Internet business are very confused about why they're there, which is why only twelve out of ten thousand business plans are accepted.

I read a very good article on venture capital presentations. It said that when you are giving your presentation, you should continually be improving it and be prepared to give it a thousand times because that's probably how many times you are going to have to give it. Many people think, well, I got my idea, I'll find a venture capitalist through a contact, I'll go and speak to them, and they'll give me the money. Since the NASDAQ crash in the spring of 2000, those days are gone forever. So, what you have to do is to design a presentation that is crystal clear and so logical that if you were to show it to your kids or your staff they would want to invest in it. Then you have to start giving it over and over again, and each time you do you have to critique it and improve it. If you use visuals or Power-Point you then can appeal to the fifty percent of all buyers or investors who are visual. In other words, if they don't see it, they can't hear it. So, they have to see it crystal-clearly and in bullet points. The reason you use visuals is so you can put the bullet points up to be seen and then you get to explain them for the listening portion. That's another thing that people don't realize—your presentation has to be both visual and auditory in order for it to address the learning modalities of all the people in the room.

TS: Now, when you mentioned critiquing your presentation, is there anything in particular that you do when you are critiquing and evaluating your own presentations, or something you would suggest to somebody who is doing an evaluation?

TRACY: When I do an evaluation I always do the same things you do. I say, "What did you like most, what did you like least, and what improvements could you suggest?" If you are doing a sales presentation, for instance, for an IPO, or even for a product, here is a great question that you can ask. The prospect is not moving. So, you say, "Mr./Ms. Prospect, no product or service is perfect, including this one. What weaknesses do you see in what I've just shown you?" That is one of the most powerful questions of all to save a sale. It comes from an enormous amount of research for which I paid a fortune. Those words can literally turn around a negative conversation. "No product or service is perfect, including this one. What weaknesses do you see in what I've shown you?" Then just wait. This is when the prospect will tell you the critical weaknesses he or she sees, the main objections, the reason why he or she is suspicious or unenthusiastic about it. It's the most amazing thing. Often prospects will tell you what you have to do to convince them in order to get them to buy.

They will say, "I don't see how it's going to achieve what you say it's going to achieve." In other words, "I'm afraid I'm being hustled." You say, well, that's a very good point. I didn't show you this study from the outside that we had commissioned, or this report from *Fortune* magazine. Let me just show you what *Fortune* magazine says on this subject.

Remember, there is a rule in selling that logic *does* make sales. People think that selling is all emotional. Well, emotions are triggered by good logic. The prospect says, "Well, I had no idea about that. I didn't know that was the case. I thought this was otherwise." A good piece of information can take a negative or neutral customer and turn it around completely.

TS: Are there any particular resources you would recommend to people if they're looking to enhance their persuasive presentations?

TRACY: Well, my book is called *Advanced Selling Strategies*, (Simon & Schuster, 1994) and it's probably one of the best books (until yours comes out of course!) ever written on selling. It's in paperback, and it really has everything in it.

Roxanne Emmerich

Our next interview is with Roxanne Emmerich, a woman who has overcome many prejudices in the traditionally male-oriented industry of financial services. She has gone on to achieve a high level of success in sales and as a professional speaker, developing a new, resource-oriented sales model. Her approach to projects involves doing exhaustive research on her clients prior to giving a presentation and is one of the keys to her success. She is highly sought after by companies in her field for good reason—she gets rave reviews. This is due in part to the detailed information she obtains from key executives before she creates her presentation. Most thank her for the intrusion later because they recognize it as key to her doing a good job. Roxanne likes to say that her area of specialization is "working with executives and leaders to revitalize people and their passion for their work."

TERRI SJODIN: Roxanne, how did you get started in the banking industry, and what was it that led you to acquire the knowledge and self-confidence to go to work for yourself in this challenging market presenting yourself as an expert consultant and professional speaker?

ROXANNE EMMERICH: I started off out of college as a lender. I made loans to businesses, and back when I started doing that they really didn't allow women to do these jobs. So I was their little token test-market person. I went to the very first convention that they held for us, and there were four hundred twenty-three people attending the convention of which four hundred twenty-two were male.

TS: You were the only woman?

EMMERICH: I was the only woman there, and it was held at the Lake Geneva Playboy Club. I don't know if you've ever had a moment where you knew that you just didn't fit in? Well, that was my moment. It was interesting because they spent quite a bit of time teaching us how to sell. But it was selling in a way that was very manipulative, very pushy. There was a heavy emphasis on how to deal with objections. I kept thinking to myself, "I can't sell this way—ever!" If I can't add value for people then why am I fighting their objections?

I remember going home thinking, I'm definitely going to get fired because I can never do what they are telling me to do. I decided that, instead, I would learn how to perfect the science of "asking good questions to find out what it is specifically that people need." So, that's what I've done over the years. Many years later I had a job of starting new banks and brokerages for a holding company. These set a few national records in terms of growth and profitability from the very first bank we opened. Part of the reason for our success was an outgrowth of a single phone call.

There was a woman named Marlene who answered the first call. Someone was asking about our rates. She gave them the rates, then hung up the phone. I was there and listening in so I asked her what happened. She told me, and I said, "Listen, we're a bank. We need money.

When someone calls inquiring about rates, they have money. So, the next time they call, let's ask a few questions to find out a little about what they need, what their goals are, and what they need to accomplish with that money." I suggested we sit down and develop a list of questions.

Nowadays, a good thirty percent of my business is in the banking world where I teach people, and have video-training programs that teach people, how to ask the right questions. When somebody calls in, we turn his or her questions around and try to convert the person from being a rate shopper to becoming a customer.

For instance, I just became involved with a bank holding company here in St. Paul. I taught them that because everybody who works at the bank has to own stock—even the tellers own stock in the bank—our people tend to stick around a long time. So, we had to work that into our questions. One of the questions we ask is, "Given that the average turnover among business lenders is every five months, how important is it to you to have a lender who is here during good times and bad times but who always understands your business?"

Once we have asked that question, rate no longer is all-important because we now have helped identify what it is that is so unique about us that they need to have.

I recently did a seminar on this for a networking group. There was a woman who was talking about teaching people how to figure out what their purpose is in life and how to find a career that matches that. She said, "I don't know how to sell this to companies because they think that people will leave as a result of this seminar, and so they don't want it."

So, I said, what you need to do is ask the question, "How important is it to you that your employees get on the right career path so you have round pegs in round holes, so they can be nurtured and enjoy their work as opposed to coming in everyday and being miserable about it?"

Well, once you ask the question that way, people see the value because it relates to a bottom-line issue. So much of being effective is asking the questions, and I think that we spend so much of our time in sales presentations dealing with objections when the reality is that if you ask the right questions, in the right order, there is no need to deal with objections. You now have figured out everything they need, what their hot buttons are, and what they don't like, and therefore you've only suggested something that you already know is perfect for them.

TS: So, are there a number of questions that you like to ask ahead of time? If you ask five or six questions, do people get irritated when you ask too many questions up front?

EMMERICH: It depends upon the quality of your questions. I think that if you ask situational questions, like "How much money do you have for this, what is your budget, when do you plan to do this?"—those kind of questions—that people tend to get very irritated. But when you start asking things like, "What are your priorities right now, what are your challenges, how do you need your people to think differently, what do you need them to do differently?"—when you ask questions at that level, people go, "Wow! I hadn't thought about that, what a great question."

Already, because of the questions you're asking, they've bought, and they're already saying, "You've already taught me how to think in a different way." So much of it is just teaching people how to ask good questions.

In my office, we have (questionnaires) we call "the orange sheets." So, somebody can be here for a week or two and be fully trained on how to use this and be as effective as I am because they know which questions to ask. I just tell them to write down every word the prospect says. They don't have to be a genius to do this; they just have to be able to read the questions.

We have a video training program that is called *Breakthrough Banking*, which is becoming one of the training mainstays in the banking industry. It basically shows people how to develop these questions in the right order. So, when people call in for a mortgage loan, the first thing they always ask is, "So, what are your rates?" In a mortgage loan, rates really don't matter much. That is because you can have a good rate and still get creamed from points, origination costs, and all kinds of incidental costs. So by comparing only rates, you still are comparing apples to oranges. Generally, the best rates are the worst deals.

We teach people that the first question out of their mouth needs to be "Are you looking for the best rate or are you looking for the best value?" because they are usually not the same. Right away the person will say, "Well, what do you mean?"

"Do you mind if I ask you a few questions to find out what the best mortgage is for you?" Then we have the list of questions, such as, "How long to you intend to stay in your house?" Well, that's important to know because the average person stays in a home five to seven years, and they are paying extra for a thirty-year mortgage.

"What did you like about your last mortgage?" They give you some information.

"What didn't you like?"

"Oh, we didn't like that they sold it in the secondary market."

Well, then you sure don't want to be saying, "We've got mortgages that we sell in the secondary market," because there you have grounds for an objection. Well, you didn't need to get to the objection, because you have asked the question up front.

TS: Do you use boilerplate forms (standard questionnaires) for the lending industry or just for your office?

EMMERICH: We have a boilerplate for my office. We have boilerplates for every division within a bank, and then I work with lots of other industries and have taught them how to do that as well. But none of them looks like another. They all have to be different because they all have to be specific to the industry based upon the competitive advantage you have and whatever business you're in. Here is a question that I could have on my sheet. Because I've been speaking for so long, I'm predictably good. Even on my bad days where I'm a two, people still think that I'm a ten. Given that attribute, one of the questions I have not had the nerve to put on there yet (but I probably could some day) is: "How important is it to you to have consistency—somebody who consistently scores well so you won't happen to get the speaker on a bad day?" (because one weak speaker can stink up a whole conference).

TS: Has there ever been a particular situation where you were in a really competitive bid and it was between you and somebody else—either as a lender or as a speaker—and this kind of process really turned them around for you and helped you to get a job over one of your competitors?

EMMERICH: All the time. In fact I was just on a program where I was the keynoter, and the less-important breakouts were conducted by people better known than I. I was thinking, "How did this happen?" I attributed it to the questions that I asked up front. When I got the program, I wanted to laugh, as it was almost hysterically funny. I thought, "Do they know that I'm nobody—certainly not a household name—and these other people are legends?" Did they miss that point? I think they realized that I was thinking on a much deeper level, and that's where they wanted their people to think. So, I won out.

TS: I think that you're making a really important point here. The determining factor between who is a *somebody* and who is a *nobody* really is a matter of perception by the buyer. So people shouldn't be intimidated going after what they want or in thinking of themselves as having a rightful place on the ladder to success because they may end up on the top of that ladder.

EMMERICH: Exactly. I was on a program last year where they brought in a speaker every month, and most of the speakers were in the range of twenty-five thousand dollars. You know I'm not a twenty-five thousand dollar speaker yet. But at the end of the program they sent me a letter saying, "It's been a risk we wanted to take for a long time, having a woman on the program, but we were always afraid to do that because we didn't know how the market would handle that. Well, not only did you have the best draw for any of the programs we've had, but you also had the best evaluations."

I attributed it to the fact that, as part of the sales process, I asked so many questions about what is going on that, by the time I got in, I knew everything that was going on. I knew what was in the way, why it was in the way, what the history was on it in terms of how it got in the way. So, I could really work them through that. They don't care if it's Roxanne Emmerich or the future president of the United States, what they care about are results. So when you ask good questions, they know that you know what you're doing and therefore can get them results. If you don't ask good questions, then it looks like you are going to deliver something canned. Whether it's speaking, or selling beans, or whatever, nobody wants something that is canned.

TS: They want something tailored to meet their specific needs?

EMMERICH: Exactly; they want to know that they are going to get a result. I always ask them as part of our template, "How will you know if I've been successful?" It's interesting because meeting planners will be the only people who will ever say it's the evaluations. I contend that they are the wrong ones to answer that because, ultimately, the CEO does not care what the evaluations say. The CEO cares about results, and the CEO is the person who decides whether they have the job next year when the budget gets tight. So, ultimately it's about results. So, even if I'm hired by a meeting planner, I always make sure I talk with many other decision makers to find out what they want to have accomplished there.

In a recent case, one of the largest banks in the country hired me, and the person who did so was basically in charge of putting together meetings. I thought, this person probably doesn't understand all the ins and outs of what's going on here because she plans meetings. So, I said I needed to have the marketing person, the top HR person, and the CEO (if we can get him), all on the phone for fifteen minutes, and I needed to ask them a few questions. Well, she pulled it together, and after I gave my speech, the CEO came up to me and said, "It's like you've been working here over twenty-five years. You know more about this bank than I do. At least it feels that way!" Of course, the feedback from the employees showed that they absolutely loved it.

You've got to ask good questions. Not just for what we do in speaking but across every industry. If you really can understand what makes people tick, then they won't want to buy from anybody else. Even if you were to say, "Listen, I just ran all the numbers on your mortgage, and you would be better off going down the street to ABC mortgage company." They would say, "Yeah, but you know, I'm comfortable here, you showed me how to make a good decision." A few rare exceptions will go down the street and say, "Oh, great, what a deal." However, most people are just looking for someone who will look out for them. I think that's what sales is all about.

What I learned that day at Lake Geneva at the Playboy Club was what I call the masculine model. Women really are still new in the business arena. What we've been doing is learning all of the masculine models, and the masculine model of sales is "push, push, push." I'm saying that women know how to *pull*. We know how to say, "Here, let me help you out. Let me see if we can figure out how to make your life better." We're socialized all our lives to be collaborative as opposed to competitive.

TS: It's a more communicative style?

EMMERICH: Even more than communicative, it's about helping them get what they want. That's what moms have been taught how to do for years.

TS: In other words, tell me what you need so I can do my very best work to help you get what you want?

EMMERICH: Exactly; we're socialized to learn how to take care of our Barbie dolls and take care of people. So why should we lose that by going into sales training that is based on masculine models of how to sell? Because the feminine model works so much better, we don't even know we have a model. The feminine model, I contend (and I've never heard this from anybody; it's just something I've come up with), is that we ask good questions. Then we say, "Based on what you are telling me, I've got an idea for you." People say, "Great idea!" They buy, and it's just that easy.

TS: Now when you do your seminars, do you actually position it that way? Do you call it the *feminine model?*

EMMERICH: No, no. But, when I give my "Thank God It's Monday" presentation, I talk about the masculine energy and the differences and how it is that it has shifted to the feminine energy. I go into it in a different way and spend more time on it there but less in the selling piece. I do use the example that psychologists tell us about the "healthiest men having a very strong feminine side and the healthiest women having a very strong masculine side." Thus, a strong man can be vulnerable and funny and child-like, and a strong woman can take charge of a room, make things happen, be decisive, and move through things. So, why wouldn't it be the same when we manage our businesses? We have to have a balance between the masculine and the feminine.

TS: Is there anything else that you would like to add? If you had to say there were three key elements that people should remember regarding making a sales presentation, the first one would be, "Ask the right questions." What would the second one be?

EMMERICH: Actually, the first one would be to understand your positioning, and make sure it is so unique and different from anybody else's in the market that your prospects say, "Oh yeah! We've got to have that person!" Second, build your questions based upon your positioning so that you get the prospect telling you why he or she must have that positioning. Third, always do the right thing. We refer a lot of business from here because we can say, "You know what? I'm not the right person, or this isn't the right product, or you need this other product instead." Ultimately it comes back to you and always rewards you. In the short term you go, "*Ow,* that hurts; we would have liked to have had the money." But over the long term it always comes back in so many different ways. One is that if you sell them the wrong thing and it doesn't match, they're not going to be happy, and you're not going to feel good about yourself. The more you take away from your self-esteem, the more you can't go out there and sell other things.

Fourth, is the niche you have filled in the market in terms of being a resource rather than merely a salesperson. You're the person they come to for information.

TS: As a resource?

EMMERICH: Yes. Always be the person they come to first even if you don't have the products they need.

TS: Thank you Roxanne.

For a copy of Roxanne Emmerich's questionnaire, "Powerful Questions to Ask People Who Make Mortgage Loan Inquiries," or to contact her about a speaking engagement, you may e-mail her at the following address:

roxanne@emmerichgroup.com
Roxanne Emmerich, President
The Emmerich Group
Minneapolis, Minnesota

Scott Friedman

Our final interview is with Scott Friedman, a wonderful speaker and presenter who specializes in customized keynote speeches that are full of humor. In fact, he calls himself "a motivational humorist." Though still in his thirties, Scott is a very successful speaker with 15 years' experience who gives more than 100 presentations to large audiences every year. That is about one every three days! Scott is successful partly because he is very creative with his clients. He sells his services largely with a marketing and promotions campaign that involves staying in regular contact with his customers. To do this, he sends out six humorous cards a year in conjunction with most major holidays. His logo is a picture of a funny bone. Prospects who look particularly promising will get two humorous gifts every year. These have included homemade barbecue sauce with a label saying, "Spice up your life with Scott Friedman" sent on the Fourth of July, or a tube of candy hearts with a funny bone in the middle for Valentine's Day. His latest specialty is a pair of beach thongs that, when you put your weight on them, flash funny sayings before display-ing his Web address, www.funnyscott.com. One of Scott's most memorable stories that illustrates how persistence pays off has to do with his booking a speaking engagement with an Idaho group he literally pursued for years.

TERRI SJODIN: Do you have one particular scenario that was a tough challenge for you where you had to go in and sell yourself?

SCOTT FRIEDMAN: I had been a speaker for eleven or twelve years, and there was one client, the Idaho Water Users As-sociation, who gave annual programs but would never book with me. Before each program I always would send them a *good-luck* card, something I do even if I don't have the engagement. (Then afterwards I send a *celebrate* card.) So, after six years of doing this for the Idaho Water Users Association conference, I cut back calling them to only once a year. I pester them only once each year by phone because my philosophy is if you can't call them up, or con-tact them, and make their day better, it's best just not to call them. So, I would only call them once a year and tell them why I might be the best candidate to hire for their program. Then I would send them something clever to make them laugh or plant a positive seed in their memory.

Finally, after six years of this, the man in charge of booking speakers finally hired me. He brought me in to speak before the association, and after the program was over, he said to me, "I can't thank you enough—and you even did a good job! Thank you for doing a good job."

I was a little surprised by his comment, so I looked at him and said, "Did you not expect me to do a good job?"

He said, "To tell you the truth, our board was real worried because you didn't have any agriculture experi-ence. But I told him that 'this guy has been sending me stuff for six years, and I can't tell him no one more year. So, if we have a year where the speaker isn't as good, hey, we will just have one bad year, and next year we will worry about it.' So, the fact that the board really liked your presentation was just a bonus."

It is not necessarily one thing that I did in that case but all the things that I do. I think it has happened in many cases where the law of reciprocity comes into play. After you do enough for somebody, they think, "Okay, now I really should give this person a chance."

TS: Had you already established a rapport with this person prior to sending them all of this stuff?

FRIEDMAN: In order to get on the list to receive a card you don't have to do much. You just have to be a potential prospect. We will have talked to you on the phone at some point. But to get on the A list there has to be some rapport—a good conversation, or the fact that you have asked to see my video or showed some kind of interest giving us the feeling that we are a viable candidate for the next years' engagement.

TS: Have you ever been in a scenario where you kept working with somebody and you kept sending him or her all of this material, and the person called you up and said, "Scott, we are really stuck here, it is between you and someone else—what can you bring to the table that is different or what makes your program different?" and then you had to put together a why-they-should-work-with-you presentation?

FRIEDMAN: Before I got into speaking, I first started in sales in the printing business. We had lost an account that was worth five hundred thousand dollars to our company. During my first week I went to the salesman whose account it was and said, "Dick, do you mind if I try and salvage the account?"

He said, "Scott, anything that you want to do, anything that you want to try would be great."

All I wanted to do was to get the client to know who I was, so I sent him a table fork along with my business card and a note that said, "We're still hungry for your business." I then called him about a week later and said, "Hi, this is Scott Friedman."

He said, "You are the guy who sent me the fork, aren't you?"

I said, "Yeah."

And he said, "That was real clever."

I said, "Clever enough to have lunch with me?"

And he said, "You bet."

So, we went to lunch and I just wanted to find out why we lost the business. As it turns out, a New Jersey printer was doing the same job for about two-thirds the cost. So, I had a price objection. Because he liked the first idea, I then purchased a little "Shell Service Station" for him and sent another note that said, "Isn't service more important than price?" The timing was perfect because the New Jersey printer was late on some dated materials that they needed to get out, and so they came back and started doing business with our company again.

TS: So, would you say this is the philosophy behind your business and why you do the creative things you do in order to get in the door?

FRIEDMAN: I think I do it to differentiate myself in a way that truly connects my personality with the client. It is doing something unique that resonates with them in a way that they remember who you are.

TS: It is kind of a combination of scouting out the right prospects, then doing something creative to capture their attention, all the while staying in front of them to maintain your visibility and keep their interest piqued. While most other people will quit, you stay consistent.

FRIEDMAN: I think the last thing, Terri, is probably the most important thing. After four or five years, when everyone has given up after two or three tries, people are still on my list and are still receiving clever things from me. I think also that it is the continuous follow-up that creates a feeling of inequity. It also helps that you're being clever and attaching your personality to what you do. Once people see your personality, they stop reacting to the proposition and start reacting to the personality.

TS: What is your most creative selling proposition? Why should somebody hire Scott Friedman for one of their meetings?

FRIEDMAN: Because they are guaranteed to get a program that is unique to their organization. I custom design everything that I do. Even though they get my proven stories that I may have used in another speech, what makes it unique for them is that I create an experience where I bring customized humor I've written for that particular group and that particular time. I create an experience that is not just an off-the-shelf program but one that incorporates what they are going through—their challenges, trends in the industry, key players whom I can poke a little fun at in a positive way, and some tools and techniques that they can walk away with that will make a difference.

TS: How do you do that? Once you have gotten the booking, what kinds of measures do you take in order to do that customization?

FRIEDMAN: The first thing I do is send out a preprogram questionnaire which is several pages. It is not overwhelming, but at the same time it does take a little bit of time. Once I get that back, then I have a sense of what they do. I go to their Web site, or I do some research on the Internet, or read through their annual reports to find out a little bit more about the company. Then I ask for the names of a few major players in the company or in their industry from whom I can get some additional information. Or I might send out a questionnaire to everybody who will be attending. I do a fair amount of work over in Singapore, and I do that sort of questionnaire over there because I need to find out who these people are from the standpoint that I can understand. So, if it is a new industry, or there is information that I am not quite sure about, I will send a form out to everybody. Otherwise, I will just talk to a few key players. I will find out what they need to know—where the industry is going.

Next, I will find a way to add some humor. I have

written humor for many years, and I also work with a comedian. We will take the situations and then brainstorm some creative ideas.

TS: In summary, what do you think are the most important elements in making the sale?

FRIEDMAN: The top three things in a sales presentation are: First, differentiate yourself in a way that uniquely connects with your customer. Second, be gracious, even more so when you don't make a sale because it will position you to get the sale in the future. Third, stay in touch in a way that improves the customer's life. I do that with humor.

Anyone who wishes to contact Scott Friedman regarding an upcoming speaking engagement or to provide him with feedback on his pearls of wisdom may do so by e-mailing him at the following address or through his Web site.

scott@funnyscott.com
www.funnyscott.com
Scott Friedman, CSP
President, Scott Friedman & Associates

Summary: The Nine Biggest Mistakes

Finally, just to make sure you have all the basics down, let's just briefly review the nine biggest sales presentation mistakes. After reviewing the list, you will be better able to evaluate your own performance and make changes where necessary.

Winging It

When you wing it, it's very common for your presentation to hop around all over the place, lacking logical, progressive flow. It takes too long to deliver, and prospects may find it hard to follow. Frequently, you may leave out half the points you want to make, including effective illustrations, that bring the presentation to life.

Take time to prepare and practice using a logical outline. Be sure your presentation covers all the points you want to make clearly and concisely. Don't be afraid to give a copy of the outline to your listeners.

Being Too Informative versus Persuasive

It's very easy to deliver an informative rather than a persuasive presentation. The reason is that a prospect can't say "no" when you're only disseminating information. Remember that it's a teacher's job to be informative, but a salesperson must be persuasive.

Learn how to build a presentation that creates needs rather than just covers the standard needs analysis. Think *proactive* versus *reactive*. Design a presentation that anticipates and overcomes objections before they become reasons not to buy. Think like an attorney and build arguments for why a client should work with you and your company and why they should do it now.

Misusing the Allotted Time

Remember the example of the president of a large publishing firm who delivered brief overviews of the books in his new fall line? Each book was summed up in 30 seconds, and the meeting ended an hour early. He could have used the entire time more productively by building dazzling presentations on each book to inspire and excite the members of the sales team. Note that the opposite can occur when a sales professional's presentation runs overtime; the prospect gets bored and tunes you out or is angry with your misuse of his or her time.

Determine how much time you have and develop a persuasive presentation that fits within those time parameters. In order to do this you must practice your presentation in advance. You should be able to cover every important argument with an illustration and know what to include and what to delete in case you are asked to lengthen or shorten the presentation at the last minute.

Providing Inadequate Support

Your prospect won't buy into your proposal if you are unable to support your claims. Many people deliver presentations based on opinion rather than a logical argument for why a client or prospect should take action. You must be able to prove your case when confronted by the prospect or you will lose credibility.

Remember to use current examples, statistics, stories, and anecdotes to support your points. Magazines, books, interviews, and other studies can provide you with factual support that can build your case and enhance your credibility, making it more interesting for your audience to listen.

Failing to Close the Sale

It's hard to believe that salespeople often don't close at the end of their presentations. Most people conclude but don't close. The close is what action you want your prospect to take as a result of your message. A conclusion is a wrap-up of what you just said. The reason many people don't close is based on a fear of hearing the word "no." Many believe that when there is no close, there is no chance for rejection.

Delivering a persuasive presentation requires the ability to close. Remember to ask for the commitment; that's what you are there for. If you have been meeting with a large number of clients but haven't been completing that many transactions, ask yourself this, "Do I conclude, or do I close?" One generates action; the other gives your prospect a reason to stall.

Being Boring, Boring, Boring

Many professionals do not realize just how boring their presentations are—too many facts, the same old stories, a flat, boring, monotone voice. Sometimes professionals have been giving the same presentation for so long they just slip into auto pilot. In today's competitive market, your presentations must be entertaining in order to obtain and maintain the attention of prospects.

Be creative! Put some energy into it! To stay sharp, practice with a tape recorder and listen to the playback to determine where your presentation begins to fall apart. Make improvements accordingly. Be sure to use material that is appropriate for the audience, whether the audience is made up of one person or hundreds of people.

Relying Too Much on Visual Aids

If brochures, handouts, or slides could sell a product or service on their own, companies would not need salespeople. Depending too much on visual aids can give us a false sense of security. We tend to think it isn't necessary to prepare thoroughly because our props, such as laptop computers, will lead us right through the presentation. We let the visual aid become the star and virtually run the show.

You are the star and the visual is the supporting player! It's your job to bring the presentation to life. Strategically place visual aids in your presentation for emphasis of a major point or argument. You must practice with all handouts or aids to ensure that they enhance rather than detract from your presentation. Remember who is in charge—you are!

Distracting Gestures and Body Language

Your body naturally wants to gesture. Unfortunately, many times sales professionals don't realize the strange things their bodies are doing in the middle of a presentation before an important client. What you don't know can hurt you! Fidgeting with your tie, playing with your hair, clicking your pen, doodling, pacing, or other annoying behavior is very distracting and builds the image that you may be nervous versus confident and in control. Seasoned pros know you have to practice in front of a mirror to be polished. Use a video camera to tape your presentation and observe how you appear to your clients.

Wearing Inappropriate Dress

Are you making a fashion faux pas? Clients begin determining whether they like you within the first few seconds after you walk in the door based partly on your dress. Although you haven't had time to talk about your company or product, they are already deciding if they will be doing business with you. Certain clothes are appropriate for the beach, and others are fine for a night on the town. Business attire is appropriate for giving presentations. These are not all one and the same!

Many of the industry books on dressing for success are outdated. I strongly recommend you meet with a clothing consultant at a major department store for advice pertaining to color, style, and protocol for dress in varying presentations.

Inspiration to Be a Power Speaker

I hope that sharing the foibles so many presenters are guilty of—and tips for improvement—has given you not only the means but also the inspiration to become a power speaker. Committing any or all of the nine biggest mistakes can cost you an amazing opportunity or cost a sales professional thousands of dollars each year in lost sales and commissions. Do you make any of these common mistakes when speaking to your clients and prospects? When you can identify the weaknesses in your presentation, you can begin to correct them, and the result will be a more confident, more polished, more persuasive, and more consistent presentation.

The reason I wrote this book is because I feel there is tremendous magic when an individual learns how to build and deliver a polished presentation. That magic is empowering because it can open the floodgates of opportunity.

Ironically, what I'm constantly being told by individuals is, "Terri, I'm not in sales—that's not what I do!" Then after reviewing my material they go, "Oh, I have never considered myself to be in sales, but that's exactly what I do."

Every time I turn around, I'm working with individuals who say, for instance, "I'm an accountant; I'm not in sales."

I then point out to these people that they are not going to have any accounts to manage if they don't sell themselves to individuals who need their services. Whoever you are, whatever you do, nothing happens until somebody sells something. So when you say that you are an entrepreneur—a creator of products—but you are not in sales, I respond by saying you could have the greatest widget in the world, but if nobody buys it, all you are is owner of the greatest widget in the world—not the maker, because you won't be making very many if you can't sell them.

Whether you are in real estate, teaching, advertising, professional speaking, or writing, or are a member of a philanthropic group, nothing ever happens until somebody sells something. So if you're reading this book and thinking, "How can I get to the next place that I want to be in my career, or in my life, or further on my goal path?" I truly believe if you follow the principles in this book, and you can avoid making the nine biggest sales presentation mistakes, you will empower yourself to take advantage of the opportunities life places before you.

There is a song by Baz Luhrmann called "Everybody's Free to Wear Sunscreen," and one of the lines in the song is that in order to live life fully, everyone should do something every day that scares them just a little. I agree with that philosophy—everyone should do something every day that scares them just a bit—even if it's giving a presentation.

What is success? To laugh often and much and to win the respect of intelligent people and the affection of children; to earn the appreciation of honest critics and endure the betrayal of false friends; to appreciate beauty, to find the best in others, to leave the world a bit better, whether by a healthy child, a garden patch or a redeemed social condition; to know even one life has breathed easier because you have lived; this is to have succeeded.

—Ralph Waldo Emerson

Bibliography

Ailes, Roger and Kraushar, Jon. *You Are the Message: Getting What You Want by Being Who You Are*. Homewood, IL: Doubleday Books, September 1989.

Becker, Hal. *Can I Have 5 Minutes of Your Time?* Cleveland: Oakhill Press, 1993.

Burley-Allen, Madelyn. *Listening: The Forgotton Skill*. New York: Wiley, 1995.

Carnegie, Dale. *How to Win Friends and Influence People*. New York: Pocket Books, November 1998.

Cook, John. *The Book of Positive Quotations*. Minneapolis: Fairview Press, 1997.

Elgin, Suzette Haden. *The Gentle Art of Verbal Self-Defense at Work*, 2nd Ed. Englewood Cliffs, NJ: Prentice Hall Press, January 2000.

Funk, Wilfred and Lewis, Norman. *Thirty Days to a More Powerful Vocabulary*. New York: Galahad Books, August 1998.

Gerber, Michael E. *The E Myth: Why Most Small Businesses Don't Work and What to Do About It*. New York: Harper Collins, 1986.

Grant-Sokolosky, Valerie. *Corporate Protocol: A Brief Case for Business Etiquette*. ASIN: 0892744170. Tulsa, OK: Harrison House, 1986.

Koch, Richard. *The 80/20 Principle: The Secret of Achieving More with Less*. New York: Bantam Doubleday Dell, March 1998.

Kouzes, James M. and Posner, Barry Z. *Credibility: How Leaders Gain and Lose It, Why People Demand It*. San Francisco: Jossey-Bass, 1993.

Leeds, Dorothy. *PowerSpeak*. New York: Berkeley Publishing Group, 1991.

Molloy, John T. *John T. Molloy's New Dress for Success*. New York: Warner Books, 1988.

Bibliography

Peoples, David A. *Presentations Plus*, 2nd Ed. New York: Wiley, 1992.

Qubein, Nido R. *How to Be a Great Communicator: In Person, on Paper and on the Podium*. New York: Wiley, September 1996.

Rackman, Neil. *SPIN Selling*. New York: McGraw-Hill, 1988.

Tracy, Brian. *Advanced Selling Strategies*. New York: Simon & Schuster, 1994.

Trump, Donald J. and Schwartz, Tony. *Trump: The Art of the Deal*. New York: Random House, January 1988.

Wickman, Floyd and Sjodin, Terri. *Mentoring: The Most Obvious and Overlooked Key to Achieving More in Life than You Dreamed Possible*. New York: McGraw-Hill, 1997.

Index

Index

Index

Index

Index

How to Contact the Author

Yes, I have read: *"New Sales Speak"*

Please send me information on the following:
- ❏ Obtaining Terri Sjodin for a speaking engagement
- ❏ Videotape—*The Nine Biggest Sales Presentation Mista¹* and *How to Avoid Them* (VHS–74 minutes)
- ❏ Mentoring materials

SJODIN COMMUNICATIONS
P.O. Box 8998
Fountain Valley, CA 92728-8998
Or call:
SJODIN COMMUNICATIONS (714) 540-5594
www.terrisjodin.com

NAME: _____

COMPANY: _____

POSITION: _____

ADDRESS: _____

CITY: _____ STATE: _____ ZIP:_____

BUSINESS PHONE: _____

Please provide us with a brief description of the kind of products or services your company sells.

_____

_____

_____

_____